Inspiring and knowledgeable are mind when I think about Jay engaged in an iPad project within with LearnMaker. Why did we choose to invest in this project? We firmly believed the training provided by LearnMaker would develop the use of iPads as a pedagogical tool to improve the quality of teaching and learning, engagement by students and staff and ultimately the outcomes of the students. Jay makes it clear that teaching subject content through mobile technology is the key concept and it's not about the apps! This project was one of the most successful CPD that our mathematics staff received with measureable outcomes. I can honestly say that Jay knows what he is talking about and if you want to develop the use of mobile technology in your classroom then this is the book for you.

Paula Jones, Deputy Headteacher, Broadgreen International School

Jay's enthusiasm and vast knowledge has been both invaluable and essential whilst we've been learning to make the technology work for us in delivering teaching and learning standards of the highest quality."

Jill Sach, Assistant Head, Bexton Primary School

In the time that Ashford School has worked with LearnMaker, we have been impressed by their knowledge and expertise using tablets in education. For schools that are looking to integrate the technology effectively into their learning platforms, *The Tablet Revolution* book would be an excellent place to start. It is an excellent book, based solid evidence accumulated by Jay whilst he has been in schools, in which he offers practical advice on how to create an effective technological learning environment to meet the needs and ability of both teachers and their students.

> **Neelam Palmar, Director of e-Learning, Ashford School**

With a consistent buzz of excitement around school from the most apprehensive technology users, a new dynamic of working is evident. This is as a direct result of Jay and James's dedication, skill and commitment our school.

There isn't a staff member in the school that hasn't been positively affected by LearnMaker's unique approach to consultancy and learning.

> **Jo Shaw, Deputy Head, Parkroyal Community Primary School**

# THE TABLET REVOLUTION

## How to Transform Student Learning with iPad

JAY ASHCROFT AND CHARLOTTE GREEN

THE TABLET REVOLUTION:

How to transform student learning with the iPad

*By Jay Ashcroft and Charlotte Green*

Education | Leadership

First published 2016

Cover illustration by Fajri Persiano

The rights of Jay Ashcroft and Charlotte Green to be identified as the authors of this work have been asserted in accordance with Sections 77 and 78 of the Copyright Designs and Patents Act, 1988.

All rights reserved. No part of this book may be reproduced in material (including photocopying or storing in any medium by electronic means and whether or not transiently or incidentally to some other use of this publication) without the written permission of the copyright holder except in accordance with the provisions of the Copyright, design and Patents Act 1988. Applications for Copyright holders written permission to reproduce any part of this publication should be addressed to LearnMaker, The Custard Factory, Birmingham, B9 4AA.

This book is available to order online from *Amazon.co.uk*

**Copyright 2016 Jay Ashcroft and Charlotte Green**

Please Note: This book is intended for information only and does not constitute legal, financial or specific professional advice unique to your situation. The Author, Publisher and Resellers accept no responsibility for loss, damage or injury to persons or their belongings as a direct or indirect result of reading this book.

# DEDICATION

This book is dedicated to every educator out there. You are changing lives each and every single day. Never forget that.

# CONTENTS

| | |
|---|---:|
| FOREWORD | 3 |
| INTRODUCTION | 7 |
| 1  YOUR PROJECT CHECKLIST | 11 |
| 2  CREATING A CLEAR VISION | 15 |
| 3  CREATING A STRATEGIC TEAM | 29 |
| 4  DIGITAL LEADERS | 45 |
| 5  INFRASTRUCTURE | 55 |
| 6  PROJECT SHOPPING LIST | 79 |
| 7  DEPLOYMENT PLANNING | 95 |
| 8  SELECTING THE RIGHT SUPPLIER | 111 |
| 9  LEARNING TO TENDER | 127 |
| 10 FINANCING | 147 |
| 11 BEYOND THE SCHOOL GATE | 165 |
| 12 ENGAGING WITH SOCIAL MEDIA | 175 |
| 13 LEARNING FRAMEWORKS | 185 |
| 14 STAFF DEVELOPMENT | 203 |
| 15 FINDING THE RIGHT TRAINER | 219 |
| 16 BEHAVIOUR IN THE CLASSROOM | 225 |

| | | |
|---|---|---|
| **17** | APPS AND WORKFLOW | **233** |
| **18** | LEARNING EVOLVED | **247** |
| **19** | MEASURING SUCCESS | **261** |
| | TYING IT ALL TOGETHER | **269** |

# FOREWORD

Providing pupils with mobile devices is an enormous decision for any school, and it is one that must be considered carefully. If you start from the assumption that providing pupils and staff with shiny slabs of aluminium and glass is all that is required and that everything else will take care of itself afterwards because "the children know how to use them anyway", then you are in for a shock. Bringing in hundreds of mobile devices and only then worrying about the pillars that will prop up your mobile learning project is a recipe for disaster.

When it comes to successfully deploying a programme that results in every pupil having access to a mobile device, there are numerous considerations that need to be clearly thought out and weighed up - from visioning to budgeting, from infrastructure upgrades to staff professional development - and all the while keeping in mind two very important things: firstly, that the sole objective of a project of this magnitude ought to be to help children learn and, secondly, that the outcome of these considerations could well be an unequivocal "we're not quite ready yet".

There are many good reasons why making mobile devices available to pupils would be desirable for most schools, but the missing ingredient in the sauce is often the lack of a sound educational case for the use of mobile devices. This educational case needs to be built solidly around supporting, facilitating and enhancing the processes involved in teaching and learning. Nothing else will do. Put this on a poster and hang it somewhere where it will serve as a constant reminder, because, in the end, the success of any mobile learning programme will be judged on whether it had a positive impact on educational outcomes, so a well- informed and hard-headed approach is required to decide whether this avenue is one down which your school should be travelling at this particular stage in its development plan.

But it is certainly not all doom and gloom. Quite the contrary. There is an increasing number of schools who have started to explore and develop good practice in the area of mobile learning, both in procurement and pedagogy, and some who are beacons of excellence in a world where bad news makes headlines but great achievements and innovation pass us by unnoticed. Jay is in the unique position of having been involved in numerous mobile learning projects at schools internationally, expertly advising teachers on how best to apply their pedagogical content knowledge to the empowering and yet challenging opportunities of the mobile device-enabled classroom. This expertise, together with his experience in business and his keen awareness of what makes great teaching and learning, is encapsulated in this book, which is an essential source of knowledge and information for whomever is considering improving teaching and learning in schools through the use of mobile devices, so I encourage you to read on, take note and reflect.

José Picardo

Assistant Principal at Surbiton High School and regular edtech contributor *(Educate 1-to1, The Times Education Supplement and The Guardian)*

THE TABLET REVOLUTION

# INTRODUCTION

I first began working with schools on tablet projects a little after the original iPad 2 launched in 2011. My role as Apple reseller gave me the opportunity to work alongside hundreds of talented teachers and to support them in their endeavours to launch an iPad project. Not long after I started along this journey, however, I began to notice a trend: there was no clear pathway that schools could follow to maximise the technology's impact on learning. Instead, most schools found themselves fumbling in the dark. This was true across every kind of demographic, from wealthy private schools to inner city comprehensives. Almost all schools were in the same boat, struggling to capitalise on the potential to transform learning that the iPad offers education.

The most common reason why these projects did not succeed was that they were not tailored to the schools' needs. The first rule of an iPad project is that it must be unique, and reflective of a school's strengths and its student population. There is no 'one-size-fits-all' plan. Unfortunately, the schools I met tended to take the same approach, investing heavily in hardware rather than training and long-term development, with the hope that the resource alone would improve the school's performance.

My experiences as a reseller left me feeling frustrated, and I began to realise that as someone that sold hardware in bulk, I was part of the problem. It inspired me to start my own company with business partner James Hannam, with the aim of helping schools to make real improvements in learning and pedagogy through the use of technology.

From the outset, I want to make it clear that I do not sell iPads or any of the technologies that will be mentioned in pages ahead. I decided to write this book because I believe that the iPad has the potential to be the most transformative tool in education since the advent of the printing press. However, this transformation will only take place with careful planning and a long term commitment to the process. The aim of this book is to prepare you for what it takes to achieve this and enable more schools to get the impact they deserve from using iPads. Through the ensuing chapters, I will talk you through the key steps that will put you on the path to transforming learning in your school, whether you are at the start of your iPad journey or a number of years in.

The chapters are organised so that it is easy to jump in and out, according to how far along you are on your own iPad journey. I encourage you to read this book chronologically, but it is not necessary to do so.

I have drawn on numerous real life examples in this book, both positive and negative. I want to prepare you as best I can, and that involves sharing the mistakes that have been the downfall of iPad projects before yours. I have anonymised less flattering examples in order to protect individuals' identities (indicated with * symbol).

I hope this book proves useful, and that it helps shape and develop your own iPad project. I always love hearing teachers' own experiences using iPads in their classrooms so feel free to tweet me. You will find me @LearnMakerJay.

Jay Ashcroft

March 2016

THE TABLET REVOLUTION

# Chapter 1

# YOUR PROJECT CHECKLIST

If you are reading this book, your school is probably thinking about launching, or has already launched its own iPad project. If one of the thoughts running through your mind presently is *'How on earth do I get started?'* then, fear not! This is a common reaction. It is also a healthy one, as it suggests you aren't under any illusion about the scale of the task ahead of you. Tablet projects don't have to be daunting, however. If you are organised and have realistic expectations from the beginning, this will stand you in good stead.

A good place to start is to make a project checklist compiled of all the objectives you will need to satisfy. I have provided you with one which contains all of the most important questions that you need to consider in order to make your project successful. To be clear, my definition of a successful project is one that improves pedagogy and students' results. This checklist is much more than a simple list of hardware to buy; it covers all the planning and development that must take place for your devices to change the learning culture of your school. If you refer back to this list, it will help you as your project progresses. I have worked with schools across the spectrum of the UK education system, and the major difference between those that use technology successfully from those that do not is how well they satisfy each aspect of this list.

If you consider yourself a technophile, it is possible that you are not daunted by the task at all, and are rather relishing the idea of managing your own project. Should you fall in this bracket, I would like to offer a polite word of warning. I regularly work with teachers who tell me they are experienced iPad users and want to begin looking at the advanced aspects of the technology, only to find they are barely out of the starting blocks. Familiarity with tablets in your personal life will not have any bearing on how well you are prepared to use technology to improve pedagogy, assessment and curriculum, so be realistic about whether your pool of knowledge is relevant to your project.

The most important objectives to satisfy are as follows:

| Question |
|---|
| Is there a written vision for what the school aims to achieve with iPads over the next 3 years that is agreed by the leadership team? |
| Does the school have a iPad team or ICT steering group of teachers? |
| Does the school have student Digital Leaders? |
| Has the school run a pilot scheme; either with a small group, class or department? |
| Does the school have Apple Volume Purchasing (VPP) set up? |
| Is the school's wireless network and Internet up to the job? |
| Are teachers easily able to move digital work on and off the iPads? |
| Does the school have a MDM solution in place to manage the devices on mass? |
| Does each classroom have a solution in place to mirror the iPad to the board / projector / TV? |
| Has the school undertaken a skills analysis with teachers to assess their understanding of using iPads in the classroom? |
| Does the school have a training or CPD plan in place which combines internal support and external expertise focused around iPads? |

| |
|---|
| Do teachers have a resource or point of contact to consult when they need help using the iPad? |
| Does the school have a plan on when and how to deploy more iPads into the school? |
| Is the school engaging the parent community when it comes to iPad use and learning? |
| Does the school have agreed benchmarks in how it will measure the success of the iPad project? |
| Does the school have a plan for how teaching content will evolve to maximise the benefits of iPad? |
| Does the school have a plan for developing assessment practices to take advantage of the iPad? |

# Chapter 2

# CREATING A CLEAR VISION

When I talk to schools about the importance of a clear vision, I am often reminded of an exchange I had years ago with the headteacher of an inner city comprehensive school in one of the most deprived areas of England. The school had just received an inadequate rating from Ofsted, and his plan to turn this around was to embark on a iPad project that would cost well over £100,000. The exchange went like this:

| | |
|---|---|
| **Me:** | *Do you have a vision for how iPad will improve your school?* |
| **Headteacher:** | *It will improve teaching and learning* |
| **Me:** | *How will you achieve that?* |
| **Headteacher:** | *By improving it!* |
| **Me:** | *In what way?* |
| **Headteacher:** | *In the sense that it will get better.* |

Unsurprisingly, the governing body voted against the iPad project with such little vision, and six months later the headteacher departed the school.

When the iPad was launched in 2008, it was touted as education's long awaited digital revolutionary. A study by Techknowledge in 2014 found that 70% of UK schools have implemented the use of tablets since 2008, an adoption rate unmatched by any previous learning technology. Yet for all the hype, there is very little real impact to show for it. It is not because the iPad is incapable of transforming schools. It certainly is. The issue lies in a school's ability to unlock that potential, and the unfortunate reality is that very few have succeeded. I believe the lack of a clear vision from the outset is a major reason.

The first step on your journey starts long before you unbox any iPads. It starts with a vision and the all-important question, "What outcome do you want to achieve from using iPads?" I imagine you have some idea of this already, because most schools I meet do. The key is turning those ideas into something tangible to work towards, so the more detail you can add at this stage the better. Here are some of the most popular vision statements I hear from schools:

| |
|---|
| To improve teaching and learning |
| To improve student engagement and interaction |
| To raise outcomes and attainment |
| To develop critical thinking skills |
| To introduce independent learning |
| To differentiate classroom activities |
| To personalise learning |
| To improve budget efficiency (e.g. going paperless and reducing running costs) |
| To implement 24/7 learning |
| Because a competing school are doing it! |

I imagine your vision will probably include most, if not all of the points listed. I have often thought about creating an iPad bingo book listing these vision statements because I cannot tell you how many schools I have been to that share them. I could sit in meetings quietly ticking them off as the school's senior leaders throw them around the table, quietly congratulating myself as I got a full house each time. It is very easy to talk a good game; achieving it is much more difficult. When I ask school leaders to explain what these statements would look like in practice, very few are able to answer. This is because these vision statements are blanket concepts filled with the current educational buzzwords. They sound very nice, get the reciprocating nods of approval from the powers that be, but are almost impossible to fully achieve.

Vision statements alone do not make for successful projects; clearly outlined actions and milestones do.

## OUTLINING YOUR PLAN OF ACTION

It is common for schools to skip over planning when it comes to technology projects. It is understandable when schools are already drowning in paperwork and staff are incredibly time poor, but unfortunately it is one task that just cannot be skipped. It is a false economy, because trying to save time at the outset will only led to headaches and problems further down the line. You have a choice of where you invest your time: at the beginning to start on the right path, or later on to firefight problems. This is also true for schools already using the iPad, because it is always worthwhile reviewing the original plan or creating a fresh one. Brian Tracey, a productivity expert, states that "every one minute spent planning saves ten minutes in execution." Having seen the most successful iPad schools using plans to great effect, I could not think of any better advice than this to give you.

I recommend preparing your plan by using a 'question and inquiry' approach, making sure your overarching goals are developed into a set of specific targets that get right down to the nitty-gritty detail. If the thought of more targets makes your eyes water, let me reassure you that in this case targets will actually reduce your workload in the long run, rather than add to it.

The table below shows how you can use the 'question and inquiry' method to shape your goals into an actionable plan. I have expanded the most popular vision statement that schools target: to improve teaching and learning.

| Improving teaching & learning |
| --- |
| Do you want an improvement in results? Which subjects or with which pupils? |
| Do you want to differentiate work within class more? Which levels / groups will you target? |
| Do you want students to have access to more resources outside of school? If yes, then will they go to the VLE or will you host them elsewhere (YouTube or iTunes U)? Will they be available digitally at all? |
| Do you want to improve group work? What stops students working together currently? |
| Do you want to increase student engagement? How will you measure this? |
| Do you want to narrow the gap between groups / sets of students? How will you achieve this? |

> Do you want to improve independent learning? How will you do this / measure this?

As this example shows, question and inquiry prompts further questions, many that are not easy to answer without further thought and preparation. Plan, plan, plan and you will have a strategy to meet your targets and overcome whatever challenges come your way.

To illustrate what can go wrong when you do not plan, I will share one the worst scenarios I have ever walked into.

### Case Study: Bankfield High*

*In early 2014 I got the chance to work with Bankfield High\*, a huge inner city Academy in the North West of England. They had launched their iPad project two years earlier using a parental contribution scheme and over 1000 students had signed up. On face value, they appeared to be a poster boy school for mobile learning. They had great access to technology and had press coverage in all the local papers. However, there were huge problems on the horizon for the school. The project had been the brainchild of their ICT manager, and the leadership team had barely involved themselves, handing off as much responsibility as possible. This meant no Acceptable User Policy (AUP) was in place and teachers* had no behaviour management policy to follow in the classroom. As the iPads were student-owned, there was no easy solution for taking devices off students who abused them in lessons. I heard stories of students playing FIFA and Angry Birds in classrooms, and worse ones of violent and pornographic material being shared during break times. Shockingly however, this was not even the school's biggest problem! The school had failed to structure their parental contribution scheme to financially cover themselves. (I talk about this in full detail in the Financing chapter). Bankfield High believed that the parents who signed up for iPads assumed financial liability if something went wrong. They did not, because on these schemes the school always underwrites the lease, and therefore assumes that risk. This risk turned into a reality because Bankfield did not make accidental damage insurance compulsory for their scheme. When I visited, I learned that the ICT manager who had developed the project had recently moved on to pastures new. He left no plan or strategy behind, and when I sat down with his replacement John*, the extent of their problems were revealed. John mentioned they were having problems with breakages of iPads, and that almost all parents had opted not to take accidental damage insurance when they signed up. Parents were defaulting on payments for these broken devices and returning them to the school. When the school sold the dream to parents they failed to talk through each party's responsibilities. Trying to remain positive, I told John it was not unusual for schools to see up to 5% breakage in the first years of a project, and that *it was just a blip for them that they were not insured.* John stood up, walked over to a five drawer filing cabinet and opened the bottom drawer. "It's more than a blip, we've got over 120 broken devices in this cabinet, all of which parents are refusing to continue paying for. That's left us with a shortfall of £30,000 for the lease repayment next month that the school now has to make up."

It is one of the few times I have been speechless. I really felt for John because he needed more than my advice; he needed a miracle. I didn't end up working with Bankfield High because there was nothing I could do for them. A few months later I heard that the school had just been rated inadequate by Ofsted, falling from outstanding. Ofsted do not evaluate the use of technology for learning, but comparing their outstanding report with their inadequate one made it easy to read between the lines. The project had produced a very negative impact. The leadership team and department heads had barely changed between the two reports, yet on paper it was like looking at two different schools. A little while later, the headteacher was replaced and a number of the leadership team moved on, all of which could have been averted had a plan and strategy for their iPad project been in place.

## THE POWER OF TARGETS

With your question and inquiry list completed, you can create a set of targets. These targets will give your project focus and help you to recognise when its aims of are being met. Putting a few targets in place at the beginning will make life much easier once your iPad project is in full flow. Imagine that, targets making life easier!

The tried and tested method of using SMART targets will go a long way in developing your plan further. The SMART acronym lists the most vital qualities your targets must have in order to be purposeful:

S     *Specific*
M     *Measureable*
A     *Attainable*
R     *Relevant*
T     *Time Bound*

Many schools already undertake this planning process in other areas of the school, such as with Individual Education Plans or Education Health Care Plans, and it is no more difficult to apply to an iPad project.

To begin, I will map a vision statement through the SMART process. In the example below, the target is students achieving borderline GCSE maths grades.

TARGET: 90% of current D and E grade maths students to attain a C grade at GCSE.

| Goal | Improve Teaching | Improve Learning |
|---|---|---|
| Specific | Provide students with access to a Explain Everything screencast on a school YouTube channel covering the key math topics they will need to understand for the exam | Move as many D & E grade students into the C boundary at math GCSE |
| Measurable | The creation of 5-minute Explain Everything tutorials uploaded to the department YouTube channel. | Benchmark last year's GCSE performance and compare to this. Can map against predicted grades and past assessment data. |

| Attainable | Yes. With 8 department staff it is little over an hour each to produce all the required content to supplement learning outside of the classroom. | Yes |
|---|---|---|
| Relevant | Yes. It is supplementing learning in the classroom and providing students with a valuable resource to develop their subject understanding. | Yes |
| Time Bound | Videos will be available from 1st week of May, when revision period starts. | Yes. Bound by the set exam period of GCSEs. |

Undertaking a step-by-step approach will increase the likelihood of achieving the goals you have set out for your iPad project. Once you have a series of SMART targets like the ones above, then choose one department or subject area in which to test them and develop it further. The key is to fail fast and learn from it. An interesting fact is that it takes on average six failed companies before an entrepreneur builds a successful one, and you will go through a similar learning curve on your iPad project. If you start small and learn from the mistakes, failures and challenges you encounter, before long you will be consistently getting it right and then you can easily rollout and apply the process across more departments and students. I will talk about how you do that in the following chapters.

Many schools I encounter try to jump head first into a school-wide iPad project, aiming to improve teaching and learning across the board right from the get-go. It should come as no surprise that it is much more challenging to work towards multiple goals simultaneously. The benefit of approaching your project with just one key target area, such as improving C grade GCSE results in maths, is that you can focus both available time and resources to achieving that target. Once you have achieved it in one subject you can replicate it across others. Adapting mobile technology in the classroom is a learning curve, and the most successful teachers evolve their teaching practice over a period of time. It is a cultural shift away from the *'chalk-and-talk'* style to a more collaborative and interactive approach. It is challenging enough to improve a single department, so the bigger the stage you set for the iPad the bigger the challenge you are creating.

## KEY TAKEAWAYS

- Create a clear vision that focuses on the learning goals rather than the technology. How do you see iPads transforming your school? Set the goal and then work backwards to figure out the relevant steps.

- Build a clear plan of action. Delve deep into your vision and break down each goal into its smallest components. Have a colleague play the role of head/governors/parents and ask you the hard questions. This will enable you to create a robust plan.

- Commit to the process. Make use of SMART objectives to focus in on your highest priority areas. Align your iPad project with targets that may already be on the School Improvement Plan / School Evaluation Form. This will ease the learning curve for teaching staff and aid the culture shift in your school.

# THE TABLET REVOLUTION

# Chapter 3
# CREATING A STRATEGIC TEAM

## IT'S A TEAM GAME

Imagine the following scenario: you are a science teacher who is on the senior leadership team at a large secondary school. You have been chosen to lead the iPad project that will see every department have access to devices. A few weeks into the project, the English department come to you saying they do not see the value of the iPad in their lessons. They cannot find any useful apps, students are more distracted than previously and they want to stop using the iPad in their department. As easily as that, you now find yourself caught in a no-win situation. You cannot agree for them to abandon their iPads, as that would open the floodgates for other departments to do the same, but neither can you send them away to figure things out alone as they are confessing they need further support.

*What will you do?*

More often than not the result is that the project leader has to figure out ways that the department in question can use their iPads. Now imagine that same scenario but with two or three departments at once. Any additional time you had spare is now gone!

The key to solving this problem is to have a strategic team in place that you can call on for support. Let us re-run that same scenario, but this time you have an enthusiastic English teacher in your strategic team representing the interests of that department. When the English department approaches you with their struggles you can now call upon the teacher from your strategic team. You sit them down, explain the situation and offer them the chance to really run with the technology to further English. They can liaise between all staff in English, learning what the 'pain points' (why teachers are struggling with iPads) are and how they can be solved, collating new ideas and sharing best practice in the department.

They can also offer to be the 'go-to' resource for anyone in the English department when they need that little bit of extra support. Best of all, they can share all their good work from English with the rest of the teachers on the strategic team, creating collaboration and idea generation across departments and subject areas. I have met many schools who believe they cannot get their staff to do these 'above and beyond' duties without paying them to, but you would be surprised by what really motivates people. Every school I have worked with developing strategic teams has had plenty of voluntary candidates coming forward.

Unfortunately, the first scenario in which the project leader does it all is the current norm across the UK, and too few schools embrace the strategic team concept. Project leaders end up taking on a 'firefighting' role, putting out iPad-shaped fires and resolving problems, niggles and complaints each and every time they appear. Let me be clear: the project leader's primary role is to be the strategic thinker, not the problem solver. There are real key questions to be answered when starting a iPad project that every school must satisfy. Which subjects and departments should the iPad be adopted in first? How will teachers be supported in developing the new skills required to ensure the iPad is beneficial in the classroom? What would the ideal use of the iPad be in the hands of students, and what new tasks and activities does the iPad offer that will benefit them most? If you do not have a strategic team in place, how will you satisfy these questions when challenges occur?

This is the biggest reason you need to make it a priority to develop a strategic team that will support your role and the development of the project. You want no more than ten members on the team, and if there is a reason you must have more than this number then consider creating a 2nd or sub team. Once the team is in place they should assume some of the responsibilities associated with the project. Always remember that the role of the project leader is to achieve the vision. If you spend your time on day-to-day challenges, such as apps or classroom behaviour, you will quickly find you are out of time for the important stuff. iPad projects take on a life of their own, so be prepared to deal with the challenges yours will throw at you.

## DEVELOPING YOUR TEAM

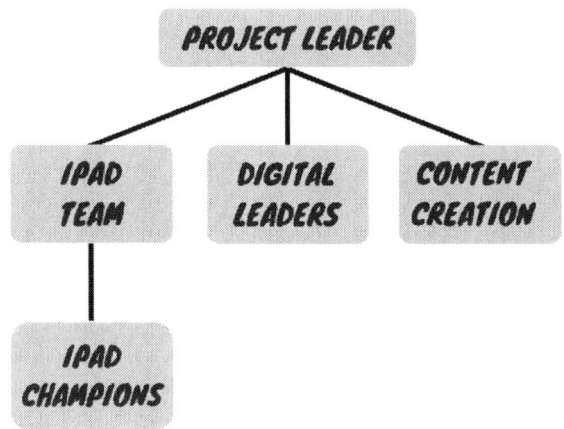

Generally, you should have no more than ten members on your team. Once you surpass this number, it becomes difficult to maintain high quality meetings. There are three types of teacher in school when it comes to technology use, and understanding the pros and cons of each will allow you to pick your strongest team. Abdul Chohan, project leader at the famous ESSA Academy, one of the most successful iPad schools in the world, uses the following analogy:

> "Imagine your school is a desert island, and your iPad project represents the next island over. Looking out across the beach, you can see it's a bit of a swim to get there. Some of your teachers will not even hesitate, jumping in to swim across. These are your **earlier adopters**. These teachers will be excited about the potential that new technology offers for learning and will adopt its use wholescale. The next group will stand on the beach looking across to the new island. They'll talk about the fact there could be sharks in the water, or the current could be stronger than it looks. This group are called **the majority**. They'll patiently watch the adoption of iPad within school, waiting for proof before adopting it themselves. They will not actively innovate, rather relying on training and instruction as to what to do. The final group, you will not even find on the beach at all! These will be firmly in the dense jungle at basecamp, safe in familiarity and routine. This group is called **the laggards**, a very conservative group who often do not see any benefit from the iPad."

This is one of my favourite analogies because it easily and quickly establishes all the players. In certain instances and environments, you may find that the laggard group become a destabilising force for your project. If there is an individual who has the influence and respect of other staff within school, they can quickly spread doubt faster than you can dispel it. I found this out first hand on a project I ran. Our goal was to develop the use of iPad across GCSE maths to improve a number of target competencies highlighted and set by the leadership team. The department was nicely balanced with two experienced senior leadership level teachers, a number of mid-career, enthusiastic and passionate teachers and two New Qualified Teachers (NQTs) in their early twenties. If you had guessed that the laggards were the senior or mid-career staff, as you might expect, then you would have been wrong. It was actually the NQTs, both fresh out of University, and part of the 'technology generation.' They ended up being a huge anchor on the project, questioning everything we put forward and slowing the momentum. The project overall was a huge success, and it went on to make the NAACE Impact Awards shortlist for 'Best Use of Technology in a Secondary School.' However, I saw the lost opportunities for the school having been there first-hand, and we were not able to establish the blended learning environment we knew would take the department to the next level. This was due to dissent from the NQTs which spread doubt through the department when we were not with them.

To contrast this, their head of department, a self-confessed hesitant technology user, became one of the most passionate early adopters I have ever seen, once he understood the potential of iPads in his classroom. The moral of the story is the age-old adage, never judge a book by its cover. We eventually got to the bottom of why the NQTs fought against our work at every step. Their mentor at the school was a serious laggard, and saw no role for technology in education. This, combined with her position of respect and influence as one of the old guard at the school was a bad mix. As I learnt more about the school's inner workings and politics, I saw the damage she had unwittingly done across many departments by imprinting her views on young and impressionable NQTs. Other NQTs held similar views about the uselessness of technology in the classroom.

It is vital to understand the players in the game you are entering. All large organisations looking to drive change are at the whim of internal politics, and schools are no exception. To prepare you for these potential stumbling blocks, let us take a look at the pros and cons of each group.

| Groups | Pros | Cons |
|---|---|---|
| Early Adopters | Often embrace tech whole scale, using it to innovate within lessons. Always looking for the next new idea. | Can lose focus on teaching in favour of technology. Can over-innovate, blazing a trail too far ahead and leaving the Majority behind. |
| Majority | Make up the vast percentage of staff within school, and will bring key concerns and challenges to attention. | Can be difficult to mobilise, will require more support and development, and will often only use iPad when shown or instructed to. |
| Laggards | Focused on the delivery of learning objectives and do not get dazzled by technology trends. | Can actively resist change or destabilise the project. There is a risk that they may miss opportunities to improve learning through the use of new technology. |

It is key that the strategic team has a mix of all three groups so that it represents all stakeholder interests for your school. The general goals the members of the strategic team should work towards are:

1. Share best practice, ideas and workflows that have been successful in their subject area

2. Resolve problems within their subject area and share the experience enabling others to learn from it and avoid repeating mistakes
3. Develop and pioneer new uses of the iPad in their subject area and report back the successes and failures of each
4. Alleviate time pressures on yourself as the project leader by acting as the point of contact for their subject area

It is easy to pick a team full of early adopters for your strategic team, but let me add in a word of warning before you do so. These individuals will undoubtedly put themselves forward and be passionate about using the iPad to develop learning, but what most schools underestimate is that early adopters only typically make up 10% of their total staff. If you create a team full of early adopters, you run the risk of over-innovating, setting a pace that others cannot follow, and not motivating the laggards to get involved at all. The result, which I have seen numerous times in schools, is that small pockets of excellence develop while the rest of the teachers remain unengaged and use their iPads as laptop replacements and produce no positive impact.

Some schools take a different approach, picking team members based on job rank. Often they end up with a team of department heads, which is another sure fire way to minimise impact. Selecting more senior members of staff may seem beneficial because they possess a higher pedagogical and strategic understanding within their respected department, but the trade-off is that you have individuals who are already time-poor with their current responsibilities. Allocating them additional unpaid responsibility for the iPad project is not likely to produce the results you are looking for. When they have ten things to do before 9am on a Monday morning think about which of their responsibilities are going to go to the bottom of the pile.

The secret recipe is to pick your team to include individuals from the early adopter, majority and laggard groups, while choosing staff from across the authority scale. Some of the most innovative ideas I have seen have come from NQTs and support staff who relish the opportunity to be part of something as big as an iPad project.

Likewise, individuals from the laggard group are usually the last pick in most strategic teams, but doing so can deprive you of their valuable experience. In regards to technology, the word *'laggard'* has a negative connotation, referring to someone who makes slow process or falls behind, but your focus is not actually technology. It is learning. Technology is only the *tool* in your project, and involving laggards in the strategic team will go a long way to ensuring the project remains focused on how the iPad develops and improves learning. It may seem like common sense, but classrooms everywhere fall foul of overusing gimmicky apps that have little educational value. I could write an entire book on this alone! The key takeaway is that all staff in your school regardless of age, rank, grouping or anything else have a wealth of value and worth to bring to your project. It is up to you to pick the right people for the job.

Finally, keep in mind that a place in the team is not a life peerage. The strategic team is no place for passengers, and you should make this clear to members who are not contributing. Certain careerist individuals see large technology projects as a means to step up into senior management positions, or to bolster the CV before moving to new pastures. It is rare, but I have seen it happen. The team's purpose is to create a culture that will drive innovation and inspire the larger staff body. If the strategic team is not working collectively to this goal, then shake things up so that it is.

## BUILDING A TEAM THAT WORKS

With your strategic team in place, it is time to ensure it fulfils its potential. The first thing to do is to appoint one person to chair the team. Your chair will have several responsibilities, including chairing meetings, taking votes and deciding on key actions. It is essential that the chair has this level of responsibility, because it gives your team a solid function and takes the pressure off you to manage the day-to-day issues of the project. I meet countless schools with committees of individuals on an equal par. They have no responsibility or authority to make decisions, which means that when challenges arise, frustrated staff turn to the project leader.

This leaves the project leader overwhelmed with a long list of jobs they never get to the bottom of, and defeats the object of creating a strategic team in the first place!

Appointing a chairperson will ensure that meetings remain focused on outcomes and actions, and removes the possibility of hours spent in directionless conversations that end up nowhere. It can be very difficult to agree on a course of action if no one around the table holds any authority to even *chair* the discussion. So, save that headache and have a strategic team chairperson.

The added benefit of a chairperson is that it offers less senior staff the chance to use their leadership and decision-making skills. This can be a huge incentive for staff who are looking for a challenge beyond their current role. It is wise to rotate the chairperson of the team periodically so that this motivator is available to all on the team. Your staff's strengths can often lie in undiscovered areas. One of the hidden benefits of many successful iPad projects is its ability to bolster staff retention, with plenty of extra responsibility up for grabs. A lack of career progression often leads ambitious staff to leave and in a climate with a national teacher shortage looming, the prospect of retaining talented staff should persuade any headteacher to allocate a little bit of extra authority!

To liven things up, offer team members the opportunity to throw their hat in the ring with a short presentation on why they should be elected, and then take a vote. It can be the team's first decision together and may start to bring them closer as a collective. In some staffrooms, the thought of appointing an NQT as chairperson might rock the boat, so encourage *all* team members to put themselves up for the role and then put it to a vote. You will demonstrate the possibility that less senior staff can take on important roles and at the same time remove yourself from any potential controversy by making it a democratic decision.

Now that your team is on its way to having its first elected leader, it is time to draw up the objectives that they should begin working towards. These should be general, encompassing objectives from which the team will act upon and further define. Successful teams have the following key objectives:

- To facilitate the sharing of best practice
- To investigate and innovate new ideas for how to use the iPad for learning
- To support the teaching body as they adopt the iPad

With objectives defined, you will need to designate a regular meeting place for your team at scheduled times. Your job is to remove as many barriers for them to reach their objectives as possible, and a good place to start is to find them a reliable meeting spot. Next, schedule a regular catch up with the team at set intervals. It may not always be possible to attend all meetings, so from the outset manage their expectations that this may be the case. The timeframe is at your discretion. I have seen strategic teams meet up weekly and others who catch up once per month. There was little difference in what both accomplished; the key was the quality of their meetings. To ensure high quality meetings, develop a set format yourself but allow it to be open for innovation from the team as time progresses. It should include discussions around some of the following elements:

- Presentation of new ideas / apps / workflows for the group
- Discussion of ideas that have been piloted in lessons / departments
- Updates on department use. i.e. who is doing well and why, and who may need additional support
- Collective decisions on resolving problems and challenges that have been flagged by teachers
- The development of learning resources for iPad lessons

There is no right or wrong format for these meetings to follow. The only cast-iron rule is that they must not descend into moan-a-thons or become bogged down by the worries and anxieties around teething problems. They need to remain solution-focused and time-managed. If there are anxieties within the team, schedule time to discuss this towards the end of the agenda, so that emotion does not hijack the meetings. Your team should be developing a positive environment and getting hands on. It should be enjoyable! Ideas and enthusiasm are critical to developing the rest of your staff body.

## KEY TAKEAWAYS

- Do not go it alone, instead develop a strategic team. Ensure you have representation from all relevant stakeholders around the school in your team to maximise its effectiveness.

- Assign responsibility, resources and expectations. Your strategic team is there to decrease your workload and lead innovation from within the staff body. Allocate responsibility to those who will be leading and have regular check-ins to see how progress is going. Ensure your team has a dedicated area and time in which they can meet and share best practice. Your job is to remove as many obstacles for them as possible.

- Keep your team small, and if necessary create multiple workgroups. Any more than ten members will stifle teamwork and innovation. Smaller teams work better towards innovation as all members have a role to play. There is no space for passengers.

## Chapter 4

# DIGITAL LEADERS

Amidst the culture of cuts and staff shortages, it may encourage you to know that every school is sitting on a huge, untapped resource of free support and expertise. It benefits from years of experience with technology and, if properly utilised, can be the difference between a project scraping by and being a landmark success. What is this amazing resource I speak of? Your students, of course! To kick start a grassroots movement, I recommend selecting *digital leaders*, students charged with supporting teachers and peers within the classroom. Lean on their knowledge of technology to make your project something to be really proud of.

Digital leaders are students who are responsible for training and supporting peers and teachers, as well as troubleshooting issues. If the thought of assigning a role like this to your students leaves you feeling wary, bear in mind the many opportunities for responsibility students already have, such as prefects and student council members. An iPad project offers another excellent opportunity to broaden their skills and boost their confidence.

You will first need to consider the specific duties of the Digital Leaders. Some of the most common that I have seen in schools are:

- Supporting teachers with troubleshooting issues in the classroom
- Finding and testing new apps or workflows
- Training and supporting staff, students, parents and governors

Once you have settled on their responsibilities, you will need to assemble your team. You will want at least one Digital Leader per class, but ideally you should plan to have three or four, because the last thing you want is one Digital Leader spending their entire lesson troubleshooting and supporting their peers to the detriment of their own learning. When it comes to assembling the team, the selection process should be open to any and all students. Students tend to take their Digital Leader responsibilities more seriously when they have had to work for the role by going through a student vote or council process. It can be tempting to pick the students who you think would be strong and trustworthy, but you would be missing out on a huge opportunity to engage and motivate other students. I have been to many schools were the Digital Leader role has transformed a disinterested student into model pupil.

### Case Study: Invicta Primary School

*When I worked with London based Invicta Primary School, we tested the idea that any child can be trusted with responsibility by picking students from across the ability and behaviour range. One particular Year 5 student on the Digital Leader team had a very mixed behaviour record in the classroom, but within a week he was a child transformed! The Digital Leaders were trained through a project based week long challenge that saw them design, programme and release an iPad app for the school. One of the key tasks was to film a video introduction with the headteacher, and this particular student jumped straight into that responsibility. He assigned roles such as director, camera person and sound recordist to younger students, wrote a script for the headteacher and even had the belief to stop the recording half way through because the script needed some rewrites! All this from a student who had barely engaged in any English or literacy lessons throughout his time at the school. The project gave him the opportunity to see that he was far more than just a misbehaving student.*

Behavioural turnarounds occur because responsibility and self-belief are two of the most powerful motivators, and sometimes a new purpose or boost in confidence is all a particular student may need to nudge them back onto the straight and narrow. Digital Leader teams are a perfect opportunity for this and I would recommend embracing them in your own school.

When it comes to selecting students for the team, I am a big believer in having a student election process (by class, unless you are really brave and want the campaign trail everywhere). It adds another level of excitement and expression for students to involve themselves with. I have cherry-picked the most successful elements from Digital Leader elections from the schools I have visited over the years and listed them below.

- Students give a short presentation, no longer than one minute, on why they should be chosen
- The selection process is by committee, which can be solely students or also include staff
- A Q&A session where applicants answer predefined questions about their view on communication and support. With enough practice anyone can craft a good speech, even young children, so it is important to assess their ability in the two competencies that are key for a successful Digital Leader

- Any student can put themselves forward. I have witnessed children with long histories of behaviour problems transform into model students after they have been chosen as a Digital Leader.

## LEADING FROM THE FRONT

Do not be fooled by the misconception that all students are natural learners when it comes to technology. You may have seen the term *'digital native'* used to define children born after the rise of mobile technology. Students who grow up with access to digital technology will be more adept at navigating devices, but that does not mean they can learn independently without a teacher's instructions. There is endless content online for students to consume today, but it is rare for a child to possess the internal frameworks required to teach themselves.

I have developed and run projects that have put the principles of the *'digital native'* to the test with primary schools. I found that students can learn independently but they do this best when teachers frame the activity and ground it in sound pedagogical reasoning. You can produce strong and independent learners with the use of mobile technology, but this comes through sustained guidance and development. It does not happen overnight and it not something that young children are born with.

With that in mind, no teacher should feel threatened or worried about using technology in the classroom. While students possess skills that are heavily stacked in operating and navigating technology devices, this gives them no advantage when it comes to teaching themselves. Rather than worrying about becoming obsolete to technology, as some teachers might, I would argue that teachers are more important than ever before, because despite the explosion of technology that young people have access to, without sound pedagogical underpinning from a good teacher, that technology amounts to very little.

Moving into the world of mobile learning is a cultural shift in the classroom. When you first start, lessons initially can be more difficult to manage as activities that require any form of content creation take a little practice to master. During this initial period, however, it is vital that teachers do not get bogged down troubleshooting technical questions (such as how to connect to WiFi, how to update apps etc.). Having the ability to call on *'technology experts'* in the form of your own Digital Leaders is key as it enables you to solve technical classroom issues without compromising the lesson. More importantly, it does not require you to spend countless hours becoming an expert yourself with the technology. Children entering their first year of schooling may already have hundreds of hours of experience using a mobile device. Compare this against the handful of school training days you receive and the spare time you can put aside to practice using an iPad yourself. As the saying goes, if you can't beat them, join them, so do yourself a favour and start using your students' collective knowledge to troubleshoot in your classroom.

## CRAFTING DIGITAL LEADER RESPONSIBILITIES

The primary role of your Digital Leaders is to support students and staff within the classroom, and to communicate information about new apps, workflows or developments on the project. There are many ways to do this, so here is some best practice I have seen first-hand:

- Set a minimum number of Digital Leaders per class. 4 seems to be about right
- Allocate one Senior Digital Leader per class whose job it is to communicate new apps, workflows and developments on the project
- Set up a 'Genius Bar' that runs each lunchtime for students and staff to drop by and get help. This should be staffed by 1 Senior Digital Leader and a number of regular Digital Leaders
- Develop a Digital Leader training program to support their on-going development. The more frequently this happens the better

- Set up an online forum for all Digital Leaders to communicate and develop best practice. Edmodo or Google Groups are popular for this type of activity. Key members of the teaching team should also be included in this. Ensure good work is praised to create a culture of innovation
- Challenge them! Refer any staff questions or queries into the Digital Leader forum. This is what your Digital Leaders are for, and even if you feel you can answer it quickly, always remember that, as project leader, it is your job to steer the ship and not man the sails

## KEY TAKEAWAYS

- Students may be more proficient and confident with iPads than teachers, but it gives them no advantage for learning independently. The teacher's input is invaluable in this process.

- Appoint Digital Leaders and do not shy away from giving them responsibilities. This will alleviate pressure on teachers to master the new technology while keeping their standards of teaching high. It will also engage students at a grassroots level across the school.

- Step back once your Digital Leaders are up and running. It can be tempting to answers basic questions or give straightforward advice when staff come to you, but always direct them to your Digital Leaders group. If you do not commit to the process and put your trust in the Digital Leaders neither will your staff. Entrusting your Digital Leaders with these duties will alleviate pressure on you and allow you to continue steering the project.

# THE TABLET REVOLUTION

# Chapter 5
# INFRASTRUCTURE

Make no mistake, your technical infrastructure has the power to make or break your project. Ground work needs to be laid in critical areas before you launch any iPads into school. Without reliable WiFi, the correct app purchasing method, and teacher friendly audio visual setups in each classroom, your school will get very little, if any, benefit from its iPads.

This chapter takes an in-depth look at all of the technical aspects to consider when planning your project.

## CHECKING YOUR PORTS ARE OPEN

Just imagine, the day finally arrives when your iPads are delivered to school. You unbox them, only to find that a range of functions do not work, such as app deployment, AirPlay, Messages and FaceTime. Do you wring your hands in frustration, find someone to shout down the phone at, palm the responsibility of sorting it out onto someone else? No need! This is a common occurrence, and it is almost always solved by checking your Internet ports are open. Ports are exactly what they sound like, a virtual dock that allows services in or out. For example, if the port that is required for the app deployment service is closed, then apps will not deploy. It is as simple as that.

Most of the port 'rules' for UK schools were drawn up around the turn of the millennium, when technology did little more than access the Internet or storage. Apple technology, because of the range of functions it has, requires a wider range of port use and you will need to check these ports are open on your network. You can do this manually by getting hold of the port list from the Apple support communities (Google: Apple required port list) or you can take the easier option like I do and use an iPhone app called Services Test. Download the app, connect your iPhone to your chosen network and run the test. This will give you a traffic light rating on each required port and in less than a minute you will know what needs to be opened.

## WIRELESS NETWORK

iPads are solely reliant on wireless Internet, which means if you do not have a robust wireless system in place you are in for a bad time once they go into classrooms. I will say that again: iPads are *solely reliant* on wireless Internet. This means that a lack of coverage or capacity will render your iPads useless, and with it, all of your planning, hard work, and preparation. It is a great cause of sadness and frustration to me that the majority of projects I see fail on this point alone.

All too often, schools cut corners in order to save costs when it comes to wireless systems, selecting the cheapest option available. This is a terrible error and cannot be easily rectified. Once installed, there is little you can do to improve a system's performance without a major overhaul or upgrade. Therefore it is wise to spend a little time investigating your current wireless system prior to deploying any devices.

The difficulty with wireless Internet is that no one really seems to know how it works. I have visited some schools where the Internet has taken on an almost transcendental role, with teachers sat in the staffroom praying to this mystical deity for a bumper harvest of WiFi before the bell goes. In case appealing to the WiFi gods do not reap results, here is some information that should help to demystify wireless.

## CAPACITY VS COVERAGE

In a meeting with the first school I ever worked with, I asked, "What's your wireless like?" They replied, "The best!" *Great* I thought. *No need to worry.* However, when I met the second school, and the third, fourth and fifth, and they all also said "The best!" I knew something was up. I later found out that when the network was installed, whoever installed it (the council, the sales company or the academy chain) had declared *'It is the best network available'* to avoid a prolonged discussion with the school.

Unfortunately, your WiFi network is probably not as good as you have been led to believe. I am not a fan of breaking bad news, but it is better said now than after your school has committed significant money into an iPad project. A second reason to take another look at your current network is that the goalposts for wireless quality have moved in the last few years. Even if your school network was state of the art when it was installed, it is not any longer. Let me explain why in more detail.

**Coverage** describes the areas in your building in which students and teachers can access the network. The greater the coverage, the more areas in your building where wireless Internet is available.

**Capacity** is the amount of data that can be sent wirelessly at one time. With advances in wireless technology, coverage is no longer the key concern that it used to be. Capacity is the new challenge, because the Internet is now full of multimedia content such as audio, images and videos. This means the average Internet page, packed with all this multimedia content requires a lot more data to load, so this means your network needs to be able to cope with sending **a lot** of data wirelessly.

Capacity is like a road full of cars; the cars in this analogy are the data. The bigger and better the road, the faster the cars will reach their destination. On a single lane road, the journey is slower and the cars arrive one at a time. On a motorway, the same volume of traffic will move faster because it is spread over several lanes. In other words, the more capacity your school has, the more audio, images and videos your students will be able to access in good time.

Even the most basic modern web page will have images on it, and when you have a class of thirty students browsing, the network is downloading images and data, and sending them wirelessly to each iPad in your class. If several classrooms are using their iPads, you may have hundreds of devices requesting data on your network all at the same time. This all means that without good capacity, your network simply will not cope.

The job of finding out the capacity of your network does not fall upon you. This requires a professionally trained IT technician to investigate and analyse your network. Often schools come to rely on the insight of the sales company called in to upgrade their wireless network. Not all sales companies are trained to the same quality, but all of them stand to gain substantial profits from selling and installing wireless networks to you. One of your most important tasks as the project leader is to weed out the professionals from the pretenders. When dealing with sales companies, ask for accreditations, and bring up the issue of capacity in your first conversation with them. If their answers are woolly and leave you unsure, walk away and find someone else. The good thing about sales companies is that there is no shortage of them!

## WIRELESS CARD RATINGS

Your network is a system built from access points that are placed around the school. A good way to think about this is as a spider web. Your access points act as the strong support threads running across the entire web, while the WiFi signal is represented by the radial strands filling in the web.

# THE TABLET REVOLUTION

The more threads and strands a web has, the stronger it will be. This is the same principle for wireless networks. However, not all access points are equal, as they are packed full of different technology. By selecting wireless access points with a better antenna for example, you increase the speed at which your iPads can download data. The better the access point, the more it will cost, so it is a balancing act of getting the best system with your budget. There are a number of things to take into consideration when deciding how to spend the budget. As with all things highly technical, wireless connectivity speeds are rated in a not-so-straightforward lettering system. Each letter is preceded by 802.11 which in technical terms is called a standard. This is a classification system, similar to the numbers you see on the side of any library book using the international classification system.

One element to understand is what *mbps* means. This stands for megabit per second and is the standard unit for wireless speed. A news-based web page will require anywhere 1-3 mbps to load in good time. Streaming video in high definition requires between 7-10 mbps and online console gaming requires 15 mbps. The speed of the access point is shared between all the devices connected. In reality there are many more factors determining what speed each device is capable of achieving, but we will leave that to the professional IT technician to figure out!

| Rating | Description |
|--------|-------------|
| B | Access points for wireless B are no longer manufactured but you will still find it comes standard on all, so it supports legacy (older) hardware. It supports a transfer speed of 11 mbps. |
| G | Wireless G supports a transfer speed of 54mbps. A significant speed improvement over the B rating. This is typically the speed of your home wireless access point. |

| N | Wireless N supports a transfer speed of 300mbps with antennae, but with advances in the antenna technology, it is able to run 3 antennae simultaneously, which gives it a top speed of 450mbps. The key for wireless N access points is that you can add additional antennae at a later date. B and G access points do not have this functionality, which means a number of years down the line you may need to replace the whole unit as it has become obsolete. The other big factor is that it also has an improved signal range from wireless G. Not only would you see faster transfer speeds within school, but you would also require fewer access points than a wireless G system. |
|---|---|
| AC | The newest and most cutting edge wireless standard brings gigabit WiFi into play. Gigabit is equal to 1000 mbps, and it is the typical speed you experience when you hardwire a modern desktop computer to the Internet with an Ethernet cable. That is an important distinction to remember, as only the latest wireless system will match the speed of any modern hardwired computers in your school. AC also has a greater range again over N rated access points, meaning potentially less access points to buy. |

It is OK to feel a little overwhelmed. I did the first time I learnt about wireless. The important point to take away is that the total cost is not always apparent because it is rarely a like-for-like comparison between systems. For example, you may need 50 access points on a wireless G system to cover your school, yet you may only need 25 access points on a wireless AC system. While the access points for the AC system will be more expensive, you will save money on installation and configuration costs because there is less hardware to install. That can save you £800 or more per day as that type of work is highly specialised. Sometimes, the savings are not always as apparent. This is where you need to think about lifespan, otherwise you may end up purchasing a cheaper option that ends up being a false economy. I highlight this in the table below.

| Network Option | Wireless G | Wireless AC |
| --- | --- | --- |
| Cost | £15,000 | £20,000 |
| Example Lifespan | 5 | 8 |
| Cost per Year | £3000 | £2500 |

In the USA, technology life-cycles play a big role in purchasing and it is commonplace for schools to have a refresh plan when it comes to their equipment. They know at a pre-agreed date when they will replace their technology, and this is planned and accounted for in their budgets. This does not happen in the UK, where it is more typical to run technology until it simply ceases to function before it is refreshed. This not only leads to a loss of educational value for the technology in question, but it leads to much bigger spending over the long run for the school.

My recommendation is to invest in the best access points you can, even if it means cutting back in other areas for a year. Wireless networks are a one shot deal, and there is little that can be done to upgrade them once they have been installed.

## LOAD BALANCING

A less vital aspect of a wireless system, but one still worth knowing about is load balancing. Newer access points have a greater coverage range, which means you no longer need one in each classroom. This means that an iPad will be able to receive signal from a number of access points within range. You will not see which access point it is connected to, as the system takes care of this technical detail. You only see the network name. Imagine you are in a classroom and thirty iPads are trying to access a YouTube video. They all ping (ask) the nearest access point and request to download the data for the video. If your network supports load balancing, it will assess whether these iPads could be shared to another access point within range. It finds one nearby with only five users on and diverts some of your class's iPads to that one. The benefit of this is that it manages your network traffic (number of devices on the network), reducing the time it takes for devices to access the Internet. Think of this as driving to a destination that has two equal distance routes. If everyone drives route A traffic is congested and slow. The optimal result is that once route A is at full capacity, all other drivers take route B. The result is exactly the same in your school with load balancing.

## AUDIO / VISUAL SETUP

With the wireless network taken care of, let us take a look at what is happening 'front of house.' One of the greatest opportunities the iPad presents in the classroom is in its ability to free the teacher from the front of the room. All iPads have AirPlay built in, which allows the device to be wirelessly mirrored to a second display. Having AirPlay setup in the classroom will greatly enhance the teaching experience. Teachers will be free to present from anywhere in the room, improving interaction for students and making behaviour management easier, while students themselves can more easily share and present their work back. It really is a must for any iPad project. Here are your options.

## AIRPLAY VIA HARDWARE SOLUTIONS

The most stable solution involves buying a small piece of hardware called Apple TV. This acts as a wireless receiver for your iPad (also for Apple Macs too), and once connected, allows you be AirPlay from anywhere within the room.

Putting Apple TVs into each classroom is the more expensive option for AirPlay, however in my experience the connection between the iPad and the Apple TV is much more robust and consistent than software based alternatives and this is a big advantage. When using the software solutions I will talk about next, it is not uncommon for the connection to drop. Even though it only takes a matter of seconds to reconnect, it is a distraction to the pace of the lesson and this can disrupt students.

In terms of cost, a good starting point would be to budget £100 per classroom to buy and set up Apple TV. That would be at the top end of what you should pay, and if you have the right audio and video connections on your display in the classroom, you may pay just half of that. When I first began working with schools to deploy iPads, I rarely recommended Apple TV because there were so many more cost-effective options on the market. Now, I think very differently because I understand the long term benefits, the biggest of which is creating a new teaching experience. Apple TV integrates seamlessly with flatscreen TVs, and TVs should be the future display of choice in all classrooms. They are significantly more cost effective than projectors or interactive whiteboards, costing not only far less to buy, but also boasting a longer life span. These are the types of details that should go into the project's long-term vision.

## AIRPLAY VIA SOFTWARE SOLUTIONS

If cost is the prime factor, then you will want to look at the options in how you can utilise the existing hardware in your classrooms. Most already have a teacher PC connected to the main display, and you can install relatively low cost software that enables you to AirPlay to the PC (which is connected to the display). The software option comes in at a fraction of the cost, as little as £7 per classroom from some companies, but the trade-off is that the AirPlay connection is less stable. There are a range of companies making AirPlay software, and I would advise you to take the trial option on a few and find which one work best. I have found that there is no clear winner in terms of reliability. The three I have installed are AirServer, Reflector and X-Mirage, and all work on both PC and Mac. One longer term consideration is that while the software solutions are more cost effective in the short term, it does mean that you will need a classroom PC forever more.

Please note that if you opt for a software solution, you will need to have a discussion with your tech team regarding the setup of the wireless network to ensure AirPlay works with your current VLAN configuration.

## AIRPLAY IN RELATION TO WIRELESS NETWORKS

If you opt for a software AirPlay solution it is important to have a discussion with your technical team regarding the setup of the wireless network once iPads are in school. It is usual practice to create a separate VLAN (network) for student and staff devices. This is standard practice to give staff adequate Internet connection and ensure their connection takes priority over the students within the classroom. This means that if you install AirPlay software on the classroom teacher PC, students may not be able to AirPlay their iPad to it for things like sharing or presenting work. This can be a big frustration for teachers as the ease of presentation is one of the biggest features of the device. The easiest solution is to reconfigure your wireless network so that students and staff are all on the same one, which will mean no connection priority for staff devices as is typical in schools. Just another reason why it is critical to get your wireless network up to speed before launching your iPad project.

## MULTIPLE DEVICE MANAGEMENT (MDM)

Good MDM can become a game changer for any school, as it streamlines the technical management of devices, deployment of apps and saves countless hours. I still come across schools who are manually syncing their iPads to an iTunes account. Stop! There is a better way. MDM is a system that allows you to manage all your devices from one central online dashboard, meaning you can complete common tasks such as the deployment of apps and update iPads over your school network without having to physically touch any devices. There is a lot of choice in this market space (142 MDM vendors at the time of writing this) and many of them offer the same functions in a slightly different package. I will discuss the key big hitters in education that you should consider:

**Meraki**

It has a straightforward management dashboard and makes grouping and updating iPads very simple. With a little practice, even technophobes can operate Meraki, so it is the perfect choice for many schools. It was traditionally free for up to 100 devices, although that has changed very recently. Meraki sell their software in three year cycles, whereas all other vendors start with a one year license. Bear that in mind when getting pricing. Its superior student-grouping capabilities will save untold hours, making it the option for the majority of schools.

**Lightspeed**

A mid-range priced MDM whose key selling point is devolved administration. Devolved administration allows the *'super'* (overall) admin to assign control over certain functions to an assistant admin in the management dashboard. For example, the *super* admin has control over every aspect of the MDM, but they may wish to make the heads of department responsible for the deployment of their department's apps.

The other big feature of Lightspeed is their MyBigCampus add-on. If you were to cross Facebook with a virtual learning environment (VLE), it would produce MyBigCampus. The aim is to have work posted and discussed in MyBigCampus, improving collaboration and feedback throughout your school. The platform has a built-in monitoring system called Bob the Robot (no, really!), so instances of cyberbullying and eSafety concerns are spotted quickly. Finally, MyBigCampus offers unlimited cloud storage for users, solving the headaches of how to manage file workflow and saving.

**AirWatch**

AirWatch is positioned at the higher end MDM market, bringing with it a richer set of functions. These functions do come at an additional price however, so if you commit to AirWatch do make use of them.

AirWatch differentiates itself by giving the admin more granular control, meaning you can customise control over the iPads to a much deeper level. Apps and functions can be disabled at set times of the day, such as lesson time, or at particular locations. For example, you could block Messages, FaceTime and Camera within the perimeter of the school, and make them available outside the school gate if children take their iPads home.

AirWatch, like Lightspeed, offer a cloud storage solution to ease workflow and saving work. This is sold as a standalone service called Content Locker.

## JAMF Casper Suite

JAMF Casper Suite is more popular in larger institutions such as the Further and Higher Education (FE/HE) sector. JAMF must be doing something right, because Apple uses it as its MDM of choice. The three I have already mentioned are all primarily geared towards the education market, but Casper Suite is a enterprise (corporate business) level MDM that comes in at a competitive price. It is packed with many of the same functions as the MDMs I have already discussed while also bringing in many additional ones. It is focused around security, inventory and reporting functions, which is what makes it popular in larger organisations where there are hundreds, if not thousands of devices to manage.

On a side note, it also supports Apple Macs on the same dashboard console, so if you have a large Mac presence you should give Casper Suite serious consideration.

## APPLE VOLUME PURCHASING PROGRAM (VPP)

The final technical consideration to satisfy is to sign up to the Apple Volume Purchase Plan (VPP). This is basically an enhanced Apple ID for any organisation that uses multiple devices. For example, if you buy one app and want to put it onto thirty iPads, you legally need to buy thirty licenses. From time to time I meet schools who navigate around this process by creating a standard Apple ID. They purchase an app once, and because you can never pay for the same app twice, they login with the same Apple ID on all the other devices they want that app on. The small amount of money saved by doing this is negated by the time lost downloading it manually on to all the subsequent devices. It is also classed as software piracy, so I highly recommend you avoid doing it.

When purchasing through VPP, once you buy more than 20 licenses you receive a 50% discount on the app (provided the developer has opted in). That will save costs, but the real power of VPP comes into play when you use it in conjunction with an MDM. This can make the deployment of apps completely painless, as all major MDM providers build their management dashboards around VPP. Your MDM will login to your VPP, and when you purchase new licenses they will be ready for assignment in the MDM dashboard. You simply select which devices you want to receive the app and deploy it. App deployments can even be scheduled outside of school hours, ensuring that Internet bandwidth is kept optimal during teaching time. Apple School Manager, released as part of iOS 9.3 further streamlines this process.

The other key benefit of VPP is in its ability to recall licenses at any time. Apple call this **managed distribution**, and it applies to any scenario where students bring their own iPad to school, or where iPads are deployed through a student purchase plan. When students graduate or leave the school, they will take their device with them but you do not want them to walk away with all the apps you have deployed. Using an MDM and VPP you are able to recall licenses deployed to those iPads, which will then re-populate in the management dashboard ready for reassignment.

## DEPLOYMENT ENROLMENT PROGRAMME (DEP)

The Device Enrolment Program (DEP) enables your iPads to be pre-imaged before they even arrive at your school, ensuring that out of the box there is minimal configuration required. You can request that the devices are attached to an MDM, configured with all the relevant network settings and even have app installs ready to go. In reality this means that once you take the device out of the box, it will logon to your network, assign itself to your MDM system and begin installing the apps that have been pre-assigned.

Only companies certified as Apple Solution Experts are able to carry out this process, so it is important to ensure you buy from the right provider when it comes to iPads, a topic I discuss in the Finding the Right Supplier chapter.

## AIRDROP

Built right into all iPads is a technology called AirDrop, allowing users to wirelessly transfer files to one another. In this respect, AirDrop is the missing piece of the puzzle for many classrooms, enabling teachers to share work directly to student iPads. Likewise, when work is complete, students *'AirDrop'* it back to teachers. A paperless classroom already built into all iPads!

I have been to schools where AirDrop is used and the impact is enormous. I spent a day with a primary academy in Derbyshire in 2015 that utilised AirDrop as the central point of their workflow. There were no long lines for the photocopier each morning, no frantic dashes making sure all resources were prepared, and no hassle carrying stacks of worksheets to and from lessons. Instead, teachers just carried their iPad to their lessons. Using AirDrop, it took less than sixty seconds for every student to have the resources in front of them for the lesson ahead.

## KEY TAKEAWAYS

- Your wireless network will make or break your iPad project. Take the time to investigate whether it is up to scratch, and if it is not, prioritise that over buying devices.

- Make sure you can wirelessly mirror your iPad to the front of class display. This is the quickest win for teachers as it frees them from behind their desk.

- Set up your VPP properly and do not try to cheat the app licensing process. Some schools may think they are saving money buying apps once using a personal Apple ID, but they lose due to the amount of time and effort they invest doing so. Without VPP, you will only be held back in your iPad project.

# Chapter 6
# PROJECT SHOPPING LIST

Part of the work I have done with schools is to look over and evaluate quotes for upcoming purchases. While working with a London based primary school, I managed their IT procurement. The school had already sourced a number of quotes from reputable Apple resellers. The school had done everything right, but I was still able to scratch off £40,000 worth of products and services that were completely unnecessary.

I use this example to highlight how easy it can be for schools to get duped. This school are no slouches, and they have an experienced business manager handling procurement. The reality is that schools often walk into agreements with resellers having little idea of what they need for their project. This is a sales person's dream scenario! The second reality is that many salespeople have no idea what they are selling you. Most have never set foot in a school and have no experience of the challenges that occur on a day-to-day basis. They end up selling inappropriate technical solutions to wider school problems.

I want to help you avoid this by sharing my industry knowledge and breaking down what exactly should be on your project shopping list, so that you can maximise your budget and cut out any unnecessary extras.

## DEPLOYMENT MODELS

At this point I want to refer briefly to the different deployment models that schools employ as this will impact on your purchasing.

| Bookable Class Sets | The school makes a set of iPads available for teachers to book for individual lessons. |
|---|---|
| Group Sets | Schools place a small number of iPads in each classroom and students work in groups with their device. |
| Personalised Devices | Each student has their own device. This may be school or student owned. Schools see the biggest impact when devices go home with students. |

| Bring Your Own Device (BYOD) | Students bring their own devices from home. While it costs the school very little to run a BYOD scheme, there are many barriers and challenges to overcome. |

## SELECTING THE RIGHT IPAD

There are a few questions you need to consider when deciding which iPad is for you:

- **Should I buy the latest model?** My advice is to opt for something mid-range. The latest model will be packed with the best processor, latest graphics and more RAM, but in an educational setting you will not test any of these to anywhere near their limit.

- There is a lingering assumption that it is risky buying technology that is not the latest model in case it breaks or becomes out-dated. Technology today is built to a very high standard and will likely last longer than you ever intend to use it for. Just look at all those Nokia 3210 phones from the mid 90s that still work! Technology obsolescence is a much more relevant concern, but to ease any worries Apple have always supported devices into and beyond their third year. Rather than buying the latest model every time, it is much better to plan for obsolescence. I look at this in much more depth in the

Financing chapter, but in brief, you should be looking to replace your devices after the third year. The fourth year is the threshold where the technological demands of software outpace older hardware's capability.

- **What size iPad should I buy?** For student devices, there is an easy to follow rule. If your iPads are going to be used on a individual basis by students, then the iPad Mini will be fine. If you plan on using your iPads for shared / group work, then buy the 9.7" iPad. Depending on the models available when you buy your iPads, you can usually get four iPad Minis for just a little over the price of three iPad Airs. For staff devices, I would recommend the 9.7" iPad, unless you think you would be comfortable working from a smaller screen. The iPad Pro is a beautiful device, but I think it is overkill for anyone but a graphical / design focused teacher.

- **How much iPad storage will I need?** This depends on your deployment model. If you are using shared devices, and you want to take advantage of Apple's new sign-in feature that will allow students to load their profile to the device then you will need 32GB devices. This is a requirement. If you are looking at a 1:1 project, providing you have followed my advice on workflow, storage and apps, then 16GB iPads will be fine for your project.

- You should not worry too much about storage for apps, because you can run an entire 1:1 project on ten apps. I know of schools that use just five, and they see better impact than those using ten times as many. It is all about how you use what you have, and by picking apps on the impact they add to learning rather than their popularity, then you will do just fine.

## WHAT CASE SHOULD I BUY?

Invest in a robust case to minimise breakages on your project. I have seen many schools, especially at primary level, buying cases for less than £5 each online. It may seem like you are saving money, but as soon as the first iPad is dropped, you can say goodbye to those savings when the screen cracks. Apple do not repair iPads.

The best course of action is to protect your iPads from the outset by choosing a drop-tested case. I would recommend one of the following:

- **STM Dux:** An enclosed durable folio style case that comes in a range of colours
- **Maroo:** A range of folio cases that are high quality at a competitive price

- **Griffin Survivor:** A military-grade protection case that fully encloses the whole device ensuring it is also waterproof.

Your target price should be no more than £20 per case; both the STM Dux and Maroo case come in below that. The Griffin Survivor is very tough and durable, but the fact that it leaves the slots for the microphone, headphone and camera not easily accessible might put you off. There are plenty of other case manufactures in the market, but I have never felt they offer anything above the three listed above. Many have better drop-test heights or are more shock absorbent, but this overlooks the fact that the most sensitive part of the device is the screen, and this is something that cannot be protected when students are working on it.

## DO I NEED AN EXTENDED WARRANTY?

Whether it is from Apple or a sales company, I do not believe warranties are necessary. The last time I checked the hardware failure rate on iPads was less than 3%, which makes it cheaper to simply replace your devices if they break over getting a warranty for each and every one.

## DO I NEED INSURANCE?

If you are running a parental purchase or contribution scheme, then I would always advise arranging accidental damage insurance. When you run a parental contribution scheme, you are essentially collecting the payments on a goodwill agreement. Parents are not legally bound in any way to keep up repayments, and if their iPad breaks and it is not automatically covered by insurance, you will find out first hand how much people dislike paying for devices that do not work. I talk about this more in the Financing chapter.

If, on the other hand, you are running a school-owned device scheme, there is a simple calculation you can use to work out whether insurance is worthwhile. The typical breakage rate on the first year of a project is 5% of devices, when they have a drop-proof case fitted (incidentally it is two to three times higher if it is not a drop-proof case). Let us take a look at an example in which a school buys 100 iPad Minis:

*100 iPad Minis = about £18,000*
*5% breakage = about £900*

*3 year insurance cost = Anything over £27 per device takes it over £900 for all 100 devices, making it less cost effective than simply replacing broken iPads.*

Bear in mind that this is all relevant to your breakage rate. Some schools see higher rates than 5%, whereas I work with others who are down to 1% per year after a number of years running their project.

## HOW SHOULD I SYNC MY IPADS?

This is the question that often causes schools the most confusion, perhaps due to the complex advice given by sales companies. There are three ways to sync your iPads. Here is a breakdown of each method and what equipment each requires:

**1. The Mobile Device Management Sync**

Mobile device management (MDM) is the administrative area dealing with deploying, securing, monitoring, integrating and managing mobile devices

Under Apple's new Deployment Enrolment Program (DEP), you can have your iPads configured to work on your MDM system straight out of the box, completely removing the physical aspect of syncing devices. There are over a hundred manufactures of MDM systems, which I talked about in more detail in the Infrastructure chapter. My belief is that all schools should be using an MDM system, because it is the easiest and most cost effective way to manage iPads. Some salespeople do not encourage its use because they are the lowest money maker. Syncing carts and technical installation garners hundreds of pounds of profit for the sales person, whereas MDMs make about £1.50 per license. Keep this in mind if someone tries to steer you away from a MDM solution.

*What you will need:*
- MDM licenses

**2. The Caching Server Sync**

Rather than download an app or update on each device, the caching server downloads the update once and deploys it to each iPad registered on the system. This was the forerunner to mobile device management (MDM) and requires you to install a Mac Mini server. A big advantage of this method is that it greatly reduces your Internet bandwidth when you download updates or deploy apps. Due to the advent of MDMs it is reducing in popularity, however it can be run in combination if you wanted to take advantage of both.

*What you will need:*
- Mac Mini Server
- Technical installation

## 3. The Hardwire Sync

This uses an iPad cart to sync and charge devices. You will need a Mac computer (desktop or laptop) to take full advantage of this, as Windows computers can only sync nine iPads simultaneously. On a 1:1 deployment a few years back, I tested the maximum you could sync with a Mac. It topped out at around 58 iPads!

*What you will need:*
- Sync-and-charge cart
- Mac laptop

## WHAT IPAD CART / TROLLEY SHOULD I BUY?

Embracing the MDM-syncing solution can save your school thousands of pounds on iPad trolleys. Investing in MDM means that you only need trolleys that charge, which can be anywhere up to £500 less than those that both charge *and* sync. Like every other iPad accessory, there are literally hundreds of manufacturers and models on the market here. I will detail a few that I have had a good experience with, because the quality can vary hugely.

If for whatever reason you still want to use trolleys to sync your devices, it is worth noting that you should be looking for a manufacturer that uses Apple MFi licensed charging hubs. This means the hardware complies to Apple's high standards which will minimise issues arising. Cambrionix is the big name in this industry, and almost all the big name trolley manufacturers use their hardware. Incidentally, this is the reason why it costs so much more to have the sync-and-charge version, as anything Apple licensed is price controlled.

As with all gadgets, there are many Chinese-made imitations that are far cheaper. Avoid these. An old boss of mine worked with a school that sourced Chinese-made carts at a fraction of the price of the established brands. Within three months, two of the carts had burst into flames while syncing. Rather than count his lucky stars that no one was injured, the IT manager replaced them by re-ordering the same carts, a decision which eventually cost him his job when a third caught fire.

From my experience, the contenders for charge carts are the following:

## 16 - 32 bay trolleys

- **Ioxi Concepts** - Ioxi Concepts make some very good value charge carts that are among the cheapest on the market. They sell direct, and should be able to buy a 32-bay unit for under £800. It is worth bearing in mind that their products are made out of wood, so if you are worried about ruggedness and damage they might not be for you. From my experience, lead

THE TABLET REVOLUTION

time (the time it takes from ordering to receiving delivery) with Ioxi trolleys fluctuates widely from anywhere between four to twelve weeks.

- **Monarch** - Monarch make two very good trolleys, the *TabCabby*, which accommodates 32 iPads and is made from moulded plastic and metal, and the *GoCabby*, a 16-bay case on wheels, one of the most cost effective on the market. Both are mid-ranged priced and a little more rugged than Ioxi Concepts products.

- **Parotec IT** - Parotec IT specialise in producing flight-case style iPad trolleys and were one of the first to market. They offer a range of products for particular iPad models, so if you are buying iPad Minis you can save space and money by buying one of their dedicated iPad Mini trolleys. One benefit is that Parotec are based in the North West of England and hold stock in the UK, one of the few companies to do so. In my experience, their customer service is the best in the market; they take less than a week to do repairs and replacements if needed, and can often do these on-site.

**8-10 bay cabinets**

- **Griffin** - Griffin make the *Multidock*, a 10-bay sync-and-charge unit that can be secured in the classroom or connected and stacked with other *Multidock* units to make a trolley.

- **Kensington** - They offer a charge-and-sync unit that is among the cheapest on the market. It is a high quality metal construction, and pretty secure if installed in a cupboard within a classroom.
- **Ergotron** - At the premium end of the cabinet offerings is the Ergotron Tablet Management wall mounting unit. In terms of appearance, its sleek metal finish makes it an easy winner. This design comes at a price, however; it is almost twice the price of the Kensington sync and charge.

In general, I am not a fan of the iPad cabinets as I do not think they are great value for money. Rather than investing in a cabinet for every classroom, I recommend using an MDM system and buying trolleys instead, which are much more affordable. To highlight the value of each solution I have outlined the costs below. The trolleys and cabinets have been rounded to the nearest hundred pound.

| Option 1 | Total Cost | Cost per iPad |
|---|---|---|
| 32 bay loxi trolley £800　MDM license per iPad £10 | £1120 | £35 |
| Option 2 | Total Cost | Cost per iPad |
| 10 bay Griffin Multidock £500 | £500 | £50 |

## Leads and adapters

It is always worth investing in leads and adapters for your teachers for those times when, for whatever reason, technology lets you down. I imagine you will not have to think too hard to remember the last technological hiccup you encountered in the classroom. In the previous chapter, I discussed how to wirelessly mirror your iPad to a screen, smartboard or projector using AirPlay. When WiFi is poor, however, wireless mirroring may not work, and this is when leads become invaluable. They allow you to switch back to wiring the iPad into the display so you can still present material on the bigger screen. I would recommend equipping every teacher with one of the following, depending on your video input for the classroom display:

- Lightning to VGA adapter
- Lightning to HDMi adapter

I have a tech bag that comes with me on every school session I run and I cannot tell you how many times one of these adapters has saved the day. They are not particularly cheap, but they are worth the investment. They will keep lessons running smoothly and keep technology-related stress at bay for teachers!

## FILLING IN THE WORKFLOW GAPS

Moving files around the iPad is a difficulty all schools have faced at one time or another. Simply put, they were never designed to do this at the level schools need. I have seen schools try all kinds of expensive on-site technical workarounds. My advice is to instead rely on the cloud (online storage) services that already exist. Mobile devices are built to run off the cloud, and trying to create an on-site technical setup to get around this fact will be expensive, difficult to implement and limited. Instead, save time and money by using Google Apps for Education.

I am a huge fan of Google Drive which is part of the Google Apps for Education suite. The first advantage is that students are able to work online removing the possibility of work being accidentally deleted. Storage space is unlimited for education customers, and if you are tasking students with creating original content then this will be a high priority. Beyond the storage benefits, you can take further advantage of Google Apps for Education's cloud based office package to create documents, spreadsheets and presentations. By working in the cloud, you no longer need to move any work on or off the device. It all lives online instead.

I believe it is only a matter of time before every school in the world is running Google Apps for Education (or some other free competing platform). It is insanely powerful and completely free.

## KEY TAKEAWAYS

- Decide on how you are going to sync your iPads before you start getting quotes. This is where the most money can be saved, and where salespeople make big margins. Double check the item list: MDM systems are cloud based and do not require a Mac computer, but it is not unusual for the salesperson to sneak one in.

- Think about what size and storage model is best for your project. If you get your workflow right, then 16GB models will be fine for your project.

- Always invest in a drop-tested, good quality case. Breakages and accidental damage are simply unavoidable on your project, but you can minimise this significantly with a robust case.

# Chapter 7
# DEPLOYMENT PLANNING

For maximum impact, it is vital that you set aside time to consider how you will rollout your iPads before your project gets underway. The best projects always have a clear roadmap in place enabling them to deploy their devices in stages. This is important because once you start your project, you only have a set amount of momentum to transform your learning environment. In many ways it is better to buy 50 iPads each year for four years than it is to buy 200 iPads at once and not invest in more. A successful iPad project is determined more by your school culture than by the availability of technology, and when there is no long term plan, iPad purchases can create a sense amongst staff that the technology is just another fad. To get started with deployment planning let us take a look at the steps involved.

## Vision & Plan
Decide what your vision and plan is. Make it detailed and specific

## Pilot Scheme
30-50 iPads trialled in a specific subject or year group / iPad use to be targeted against measurable outcomes / 1 term length minimum.

## Review & Evaluation
A review and evaluation of the pilot scheme against the targeted outcomes / Should include the Pilot teaching group, Pilot student group and iPad Team / Successes and failures should be documented so that other departments and teachers can learn from them.

## Revisit Vision
Your pilot scheme should have brought your school's strengths and weaknesses to the fore. With this in mind, you should revisit your Vision and Plan for the larger project and amend it as necessary.

## Bolster Infrastructure
This will only be necessary if the pilot scheme highlighted technical challenges or failings that exist in your current school system.

## First Year Deployment
Deploy to your selected year group, subject or student groups

## Scaling the Project
Repeat the process of evaluating what worked and what did not to continually improve your project year-on-year as you deploy more devices.

## CONTINUOUS IMPROVEMENT

Deployment planning follows three themes, which you may have spotted in the previous flowchart. **Plan. Deploy. Review.** Getting the most out of technology is a continuous process because new software, updates and functions are constantly being released. If you adopt a continuous improvement mind-set then your project will go from strength to strength, year after year.

**Stage 1: The pilot scheme**

To run a good pilot scheme, you need to have your iPads tested exclusively by a small student group for a prolonged period of time. It would be wise to limit their use in primary school to a single Key Stage, or in secondary school to a specific department for a set period of time. This may seem counter to the goal of providing learning resources for the whole school, but to best maximise the iPad's potential you first need to understand its strengths and weaknesses.

It is better to view your iPad project as a *learning intervention* rather than a *school resource*. This may sound strange but it makes sense when put into context. *Learning interventions* are targeted. If you hired an extra teacher to run after-school maths lessons for underperforming students, but then had them teach history, you would find that intervention would fail. If a school buys *resources* for maths such as calculators, rulers and protractors, there is no expectation that these will improve student learning or outcomes. Schools buy iPads with the expectation that they are a learning intervention and will improve outcomes, but then deploy them as a resource by letting every department have access to them. This often reduces availability for students to a handful of hours per week, so it is no wonder iPads do not impact on outcomes for the vast majority of schools. By limiting their usage to a select group, you will learn more in one term than you would in a full year if you used them as a bookable resource.

Limit your pilot scheme to a specific department, subject or year group and put in place some performance measurements. These soft targets will help focus your pilot group teachers. Here are some examples of good targets to put in place:

- How do iPads aid the differentiation of work?
- How do iPads improve and/or facilitate group work?
- How do iPads create independent learning opportunities?
- How do iPads support and/or deepen lesson content?
- How do iPads impact on behaviour and/or attendance?
- What new opportunities do iPads present for the subject / department / year group?

## Stage 2: Review and evaluation

Once the pilot scheme has run its length, come together as a team (yourself, the iPad team and the pilot scheme participants) and review and evaluate the findings. Focus on the soft targets you put in place, and encourage the pilot scheme participants to put their ideas forward. Once you have reviewed the soft targets, it is important to explore the technical challenges that occurred. Make sure to have an agenda on display and purposely leave the technical aspects towards the end of the session, otherwise they can end up dominating the meeting. Encourage participants to share the technical challenges they encountered but ask them to do so with a pragmatic mindset. The aim is to leave the emotion out of the discussion, instead focus on solutions. I have included an example below:

> **Emotional response:** "I couldn't get on the WiFi most of the time and this RUINED my lessons!"
> **Pragmatic response:** "I wasn't able to connect to the WiFi most of the time, so we should prioritise improving access; otherwise it can derail a lesson."

Once the technical challenges have been recorded, you should always ask your participant teachers what the school could provide that would enable them to improve how they use iPads. This is a sorely neglected question, and many schools have no idea of the sentiment their own teachers hold about the project. It is common for project leaders to assume that all teachers share their excitement and vision about putting devices into classrooms, when the truth could not be more different.

### Case Study: Broadgreen International School

*When I worked with Broadgreen International School, we conducted an anonymous survey with the math teachers prior to starting the project. The school's leadership team were very surprised when 6 out of the 8 department teachers said they felt lessons that incorporated iPads were often worse than those that used textbooks. Teachers said they were not sure what they should be doing with iPads other than using the Internet. This sentiment was a reflection of the lack of professional development math teachers received in this area, and prompted the school's leadership team to sign off on a 10 week project with me to gain real impact on learning.*

By the end of the review stage, you should have a wealth of feedback on how the iPad has impacted on the pilot group, and plenty of potential new avenues for learning opportunities that you can explore. You should also have a clear idea of whether your infrastructure is up to the grade it needs to be.

## Stage 3: Review Vision and Plan

You should put the feedback gained from the pilot scheme into the vision and plan for the entire project to ensure it is both realistic and achievable. Your vision and plan is an on-going process of refinement and adjustment throughout your project and should never be complete.

## Stage 4: Bolster Infrastructure

Your pilot scheme may have exposed challenges in either the technical infrastructure of the school or in the educational workflow for the classroom. These generally come down to problems with the Internet and wireless system, or saving and managing work on iPads. Make sure you take your pilot team's feedback on board, and heed any concerns they have. The more devices you have in school, the more they will amplify any infrastructure problems that exist, so fix them sooner rather than later.

## Stage 5: First Deployment

Once you have completed all the previous steps, you will be ready to launch your first deployment. This is your first large scale rollout of iPads into classrooms.

## CHOOSING THE RIGHT DEPLOYMENT MODEL

When it comes to rolling out your devices there are a number of deployment models you can follow.

**1. Class sets**

A lot of schools opt for class sets, iPads that can be booked by teachers for particular lessons when available. Under this deployment model each student will receive an iPad for the lesson. However, because the iPads are booked on a 'first come, first serve' basis, students are very unlikely to pick up the same device in the following lesson. This means that work must be finalised by the end of the lesson, reducing the scope and depth that the device can be used for.

Bookable class sets are the most popular deployment choice in schools as it ensures the technology is available to everyone. The bad news, however, is that all the available research indicates that this deployment model has little to no impact on improving outcomes.

In 2012, researchers from the University of Hull completed what is still the UK's largest independent study of iPad usage in education (Burden et al. 2012). The study evaluated the use of iPads across eight Scottish schools over five months. The schools used a variety of deployment models. The study measured impact on learning against Scotland's Curriculum for Excellence which targeted the development of four key attributes that had been identified as leading to better achievement. These were:

- to be successful learners
- to be confident individuals
- to be responsible citizens
- to be effective contributors

Alongside the Curriculum of Excellence, researchers also looked at student levels of motivation, engagement and how much responsibility they were taking for their learning.

The study found that students using bookable class sets received the least impact from the technology. It concludes that the poor impact was due to a lack of personalisation for the learner (which is, after all, the core strength of mobile technology). Classrooms using bookable sets were using the iPad largely as a substitute tool; for example, using Google Maps to search for a country instead of an atlas. The other disadvantage of bookable class sets is that it reduced individual student time on the iPad. When any teacher in the school can book the iPad set, students usually only receive a handful of lessons with iPads each week. This is too little to have any impact.

## 2. Group sets

This is when a school buys a set number of devices that are resources for a particular classroom only. This is most popular in primary schools, where 8-10 iPads are typically issued to each classroom and students work in groups to complete their work. Students can pick up the same device and carry on their work from where they left off because the iPads stay within the classroom. Once work can be spread across multiple lessons, teachers can begin to implement new activities for students. The most popular of these are project and challenge-based learning activities, in which students are set open ended tasks and challenges that they must solve in their groups. Great examples I have seen of this are where students create a three minute advert for a country of their choice, or solve a pressing world problem such as saving an endangered species. I will cover this in more detail in the Learning Evolved chapter.

## 3. Personalised devices

In this model, every student has their own device, so their iPad is tailored to their particular needs. With personalised devices, you have the ability to implement blended and flipped learning (see the

Learning Evolved chapter), two models of learning that enable students to consume and interact with curriculum material outside of the classroom. These take after-school learning to the next step, and, in my opinion offer the opportunity for real impact.

Regardless of the ownership of the device (school owned or parent owned), you should allow students to take their iPads home because you are only limiting impact if you do not. If insurance is a worry I discussed this in the Finance chapter.

## 4. Bring Your Own Device (BYOD)

Allowing students to bring in their own device may seem like a great idea because it floods the school with technology at no cost, but in reality it is a difficult process to manage. I will not say much on this other than that in my opinion it does not work in compulsory age education. There is no system or solution available currently to manage the breadth of devices and platforms that exist, so you will be unable to retain technical control within school. Teachers, already time pressed, will also face an even greater task trying to plan lessons that cater for multiple platforms. Add to the mix the fact that students will have games, videos, and social media platforms installed on their own devices and you have a problem on your hands. I am sure you will see that BYOD creates a multitude of new distractions and large scale challenges that need to be overcome before it will positively develop your learning environment.

## SCALING YOUR PROJECT

Now that you have a better understanding of the deployment models available, it is time to look at how to scale your project. Scaling your project happens on two levels. First, it is increasing how many iPads you have to improve access to the technology. This is a straightforward aspect as you only have a set number of options to buy devices. I explore these in detail in the Financing chapter.

The second element is how to ensure the technology is increasing its effectiveness over time. Many schools believe that buying more iPads will automatically improve learning, but this is not the case. It is not about numbers, it is about effectiveness. To develop a plan to **educationally** scale your project, it is a useful practice to benchmark iPad use against a framework. The SAMR model is perfect for this.

SAMR, developed by Dr. Ruben Puentedura, is a model that supports and aids teachers to design, develop, and infuse digital learning experiences into the classroom by using a graduated assessment framework.

## TRANSFORMATION

**REDEFINITION**
Tech allows for the creation of new tasks, previously inconceivable

**MODIFICATION**
Tech allows for significant task design

## ENHANCEMENT

**AUGMENTATION**
Tech acts as a direct tool substitution, with functional change

**SUBSTITUTION**
Tech acts as a direct tool substitution, with no functional change

*The SAMR Model*

The thinking behind SAMR is that in order to impact learning, it is the learning task, not the learning technology that is the key factor. The four stages of technology use are divided into two groups: enhancement and transformation. Typically, until you reach the transformation stage you will not see a significant impact on learning. I will limit the explanation to that for this chapter as I talk about it in much more detail in the Learning Frameworks chapter later on.

Alongside the SAMR model, Apple created a rollout framework that is useful. It breaks an iPad deployment into three stages:

**consider, adopt** and **scale**. You will see in the table below I have mapped this framework in line with the SAMR model to give a comprehensive guide to evaluating just exactly where your project is in the bigger picture.

| Stage | Consider | Adopt | Scale |
| --- | --- | --- | --- |
| Number of iPads | 0-30 | 31-100 | 100+ |
| Info | Undertaking a pilot scheme to test if iPads are right for the school | Adoption rate increases as pilot scheme judged to be a success | iPad identified as a key driver to improving outcomes and school places significant investment in more devices |
| Goals | Focus on student engagement, quality of work, behaviour changes and general quality of learning | Introduction of more complex tasks such as content creation in the classroom. | Focus on integration of iPads into the day-to-day of school, using them to improve assessment for learning, while providing flipped / blended learning resources for students |

| SAMR Model | Mainly substitution use with elements of augmentation thrown in | Use should begin moving towards augmentation in the least, with elements of modification appearing | Use should start to target redefinition of existing tasks to deepen and improve student learning. |

I should point out that neither framework is research led, however both have been developed by evaluating thousands of educational deployments and seeing what works best. As you increase the number of iPads you have in school, logically you should begin seeing a impact on teaching and learning. Improvements do not happen by themselves, and most schools have stalled with their projects because they are not focused on the educational impact. I have met numerous schools who fall into the **scale** category, having hundreds of iPads, but in educational impact they are yet to move beyond the **consider** stage. Always remember it is not about how many iPads you have, it is only about what you do with them. Without a vision and implementation strategy, your school will not develop beyond the **consider** stage no matter how many devices you buy.

## KEY TAKEAWAYS

- Always start with a pilot scheme. This could be with a department, year group or cohort of selected students. It does not matter who uses the devices as long as you can measure the impact.

- Developing an iPad project is more than just amassing devices. Many mistake large numbers of iPads as a sign they are doing great work, but without adequate investment in staff training and a clear implementation strategy, you will not see any educational impact.

- In the statutory education system BYOD is not a strategy, it is a gamble. It may work in the Independent, College or University sector, but I am yet to meet a state secondary school where it has had a positive impact. The advantage of flooding the school with technology is countered by the many disadvantages it brings. Loss of control, no unified classroom tech platform and student inequality are just the tip of the iceberg.

Chapter 8

# SELECTING THE RIGHT SUPPLIER

Price is usually at the forefront of the decision making process for schools buying new hardware. However, getting the best value for money involves more than getting the lowest price. Most schools get hung up on pricing, (perhaps because of the guidelines from the Department of Education), and while it is important to get competitive quotes, you should also look to find a company that has the relevant expertise and knowledge too. Implementation is everything on a technology project, and the more expertise and knowledge you have access to the better.

I want you to consider funding as the most flexible aspect of this whole undertaking. You may be lucky enough to have £50,000 to spend. You may have more. Either way, it does not mean you need to spend it all because it is all relative to your plan. A school that spends £50,000 on their project is not necessarily any better than one that cost £20,000. It is all relative to the technology's implementation with teaching and learning.

Many schools believe that they do not have the finances to even start an iPad project, but I am here to tell you that is not the case. Slow and steady wins the race, and I know many schools that have small clusters of iPads and use them far more effectively than some of the biggest 1:1 projects in the country. Some schools are lucky enough to be able to afford hundreds of iPads, but without giving adequate consideration to all the points raised in this book, they will find that the devices alone will not transform teaching and learning. Availability of technology within school is no measure of success, and whether it takes you one year to achieve your vision or ten, the only thing that matters is that you achieve it.

## BUYING FROM THE RIGHT SUPPLIER

To begin, let us take a look at where you should buy your iPads. Working with the right supplier can be the difference between success and failure because not all suppliers are created equal. One of your most important decisions will be to select a supplier that can work in your school's interest: These projects are complex, and it is not as simple as getting the best price. There are three types of suppliers available to you:

## 1. Apple Solutions Expert (ASE) certified reseller

An Apple Solutions Expert (ASE) is a sales company that has been certified by Apple and partners with them to supply their products. This is important because they have access to the best pricing and offer numerous other advantageous such as the training rebates that Apple only make available to ASE partners. In my opinion, you disadvantage yourself if you buy from anyone but an ASE, so they should really be your first choice. There are numerous ASEs across the UK, so you are not short of options either.

Apple has a dedicated page on its website that will allow you to find your local ASE based on your location. Do note that it only returns results within a certain radius so you will not get a complete list of all the ASEs in the market. Search the major cities to get more options.

## 2. Non-Apple Solution Expert certified reseller

Sales of iPads are booming, so it is no surprise that everyone wants to get in on the action. Many ASEs sell to non-Apple accredited companies around the UK. This is called sub-distribution. Let us say you decide to buy your iPads from Targo Computers* because they have sold you laptops, smartboards and IT support for the past ten years. Targo Computers buy the iPads from an Apple Solutions Expert, mark them up a couple of percent and sell them to you. While you may not mind spending a little more to buy from a company you trust, it is important to understand that the likes of Targo Computers do not work with Apple, and therefore do not have access to Apple's support, expertise and research on how to best implement iPads into your school.

When I first started in sales, I won a large contract to supply Tramford IT Services* with Apple equipment. Tramford are an IT service provider and had won a seven-year contract with *Building Schools for the Future* for a county encompassing 200+ schools. Their role was to provide all IT support for these schools. They also offered a 'helping hand' by sourcing iPads from companies and selling them onto the schools (their 'sourcing service'). Taking full advantage of this opportunity, they pocketed a slice of the money paid by schools for the hardware. It might have raised eyebrows if they had put a mark-up on each iPad they sold, so instead they required sales companies to pay a rebate at the end of each quarter, essentially hiding the profit and this activity away from prying eyes.

The ethical boundary was truly broken as Tramford mandated that they would only support iPads that had been sourced through themselves while also insisting that schools must purchase a 3-year warranty (which they received another handsome rebate on). They effectively denied schools access to the expertise and knowledge of the ASEs in the market, and unsurprisingly the technology had little to no impact in these schools. I would wager good money that this broke the terms of their *Building Schools for the Future* contract. It was difficult for teachers to get a sense of perspective about Tramford's poor level of service because every school in the county was tied into the same seven-year contract. When I walked into classrooms, I found their ICT infrastructure and usage was years behind the national average, and all because Tramford had bottled-necked progress for their own financial gain.

This is at the extreme end of what can happen but the moral of the story remains. Some companies will go to great lengths to make money and schools are often seen as an easy target. Do not just follow other schools because it is the status quo; do your own research and decide for yourself.

**3. Retail companies**

Sometimes it is hard to know where to start when buying iPads. I have worked with schools who leave it until the last minute for this very reason, and end up buying from Apple Retail stores, Currys PC World and, in one case, their local Argos! This is not a good idea. Even if you buy from an Apple retail store, you are missing out. Apple is divisionalised, essentially divided into two businesses. You have the Retail business (Apple stores) and the Corporate business (everything else you do not see). Apple's education team operate within Apple Corporate, and most shop floor employees in an Apple retail store are not even aware they exist.

If you walk into an Apple Retail store and ask to buy a significant number of iPads for your school, then ideally the Apple employee should refer you to the Apple education team, because they can offer education-specific support. I have worked with plenty of schools where that has not happened, and a few months down the line when the school realise they need additional support, they find themselves stuck. Apple Retail do not have a education field team and are not set up to provide after-sales service to schools.

**The Internet**

I know, I have listed a fourth option when I said there were only three. This one should not even be on the list, but I felt it was important to give it a mention. The rule of thumb is, never EVER buy your devices from the Internet. This may be unwelcome advice, perhaps you have already seen some tempting bargains from little-known online companies offering rock bottom prices. Be warned that if you find such a steal, the people behind it will be after a bargain themselves, and are fairly likely to provide you with poor service.

A primary school I worked with decided to ignore this rule and bought their iPads from an online company called Nursery Rhyme

Innovations*. At the time I was working at one of the largest ASEs in the UK and had offered the school a quote, yet simply could not compete with Nursery Rhyme Innovations excellent 'value for money.' My colleagues and I had never heard of this company, so I decided to look into them. With a little digging at Companies House, I found out that Nursery Rhyme Innovations was registered to a very small cottage in Cornwall. Their prices were suspiciously low, so low in fact that had I matched them, I would have lost £5 per iPad. Payment was also required upfront. I passed my findings onto the school, but they stuck to their guns and ordered from them anyway.

A few months later, the school got back in touch. It turned out that the devices that were advertised as new were, in fact, used and in poor condition. In the industry this is called *grey stock* and you always gamble when ordering it. There is a legal requirement to tell the customer upfront that it is grey stock, however Nursery Rhyme Innovation did not do that. Of the fifty iPads they ordered, three did not work and a number were dented and scuffed. The order did not arrive in time for September term, arriving instead in dribs and drabs over a period of nine weeks. The school rang up the listed number and emailed their complaints, but never managed to speak to anyone and did not receive a single reply to any of their messages. It was a lesson they learned the hard way.

Another example of chasing low prices, whether it is for iPads or accessories, is that many of the places selling them online are not VAT registered. Amazon and eBay is full of Asian supplied cases and accessories from users who do not have a VAT registration. I have met plenty of schools who have miscalculated their spending because of this simple fact. That is 20% lost. The Internet is a great place as a consumer, but it is a big risk using it as a school for such an important project.

## UNDERSTANDING VALUE

*"Price is what you pay. Value is what you get"*
**Warren Buffet**

There are a range of ASEs across the UK, from local firms with a handful of employees to multinationals turning over big bucks each year. Before you start the quote process, it is important to think about the type of relationship you want from the company supplying your hardware. Most ASEs will quote a solution proposal to you, a recommendation of hardware, software, and services. These will differ from company to company, and evaluating the value of each proposal for your school is much more than just looking at the price at bottom of the quote.

Project leaders should keep in mind the microeconomic theory *opportunity cost*, the idea that when one alternative is chosen, another alternative is lost. Businesses often refer to this when deciding what to invest in and how to develop their brand. I have met a lot of schools who have chosen a supplier because they were as little as 50p cheaper per iPad than their competitors. The school was quick to point out how much they saved by working with them, but what I saw in their classrooms was students using iPads for little more than web browsing and word processing. In other words, no different to the laptops or computers the iPads replaced. It was often the case that their supplier of choice did not possess or choose to share the necessary technical skills or expertise, with the consequence that the school received no support or guidance on what to do next

*Opportunity cost* is a relevant concept because I find that, for the sake of saving a bit of money, the opportunity for improvement in learning is lost. Consider the dilemma of a school that wants to buy ten iPads. They have been quoted £2000 for ten iPads from a retailer that is unable to offer any additional support, and £2100 from an ASE that has expertise and technical skills to offer. In my experience, the school that opts to buy ten iPads from the £2000 retailer will not have saved £100, but instead wasted £2000 on iPads if they do not have any impact. This is not an attack on schools and teaching staff, but a plea to think seriously about the impact of the money you spend. Unless you use the iPads to offer an improvement to the quality of learning, what have you actually gained?

Put aside any thoughts about saving money when working through your proposals and instead focus on who to invest your budget in instead. That is what an iPad project is, an investment into your school's learning environment.

How do you assess value then? Price should never be the *only* purchasing factor for a school, but it is often the easiest because it is right there in black and white. In the table below, I have included the key questions that should be addressed between yourself and your iPad team that will enable you to assess which sales company is right for you.

| Question | Guidance |
| --- | --- |
| Do you want a personal touch, with face to face meetings for your project? | Ensure your sales company is local and even think about writing a clause in your tender for scheduled project meetings. Many sales companies operate only over the phone, and this can prove to be a major obstacle if you require on-site discussions. |
| Do you want someone with a strong track record of delivering projects? | Ask for case studies and references, and don't be afraid to ask to visit the company's projects. It's easy to create a few case studies, but are these project actual improving learning? |

| | |
|---|---|
| How much on-going support do you need? | Do not plan on your project going perfectly because few do. Think about what level of support you may need for the future. Question the company's technical and pedagogical skills within their team. It is easy to offer a technical solution to many problems you may encounter, but this may not be the best outcome for the classroom, students or teachers. |
| Is lower price or going that extra mile more important to you? | If you buy from the cheapest supplier, do not be surprised if you do not hear anything from the company once you have paid. A good value-added company should regularly keep in contact, invite you to relevant events and even help you network with local like minded schools, educators and projects. Sometimes a little hand holding can make a big difference. |
| Have you discussed unexpected costs for your project with your supplier? | It is wise to build a contingency fund into your project because things inevitably go wrong. If you require technical support from your supplier make sure you know what they will support you with before you have to start paying. Many companies charge up to £1000 per day for their technical expertise. It is one of the oldest sales tricks in the book - sell low and then price high when a customer needs help the most. |

| | |
|---|---|
| What happens for repairs or faulty equipment? | UK consumers are protected by robust trading laws, but these do not all apply in the business world. You need be clear on what happens if repairs or faulty equipment needs collection from school, as sometimes shipment costs may be your responsibility. |
| Does the supplier hold the relevant certifications? | Some companies are out to make a quick profit, and they will sell you pretty much anything you ask for. It does not always means they know how to install, manage or deploy that product or service correctly. Always check. |
| Does the supplier hold the relevant documentation for parental contribution schemes? | When you enter into a parental contribution scheme, you are underwriting the cost and asking your supplier to recover the payments from parents. You need to be razor sharp with the details on how they will collect payments, and most importantly, what steps they will undertaken if parents do not pay. More on this in a later chapter. |
| Have you checked the supplier's insurance policies? | Some insurers will not pay out if they feel the device has not been adequately protected (with an approved case) or looked after (through policies you have implemented as a school). Inevitably, you will face at least a few breakages on your iPad project, so ensure you carefully check the documentation and select the right insurer. |

Align the answers to the questions above with your assessment of your own school. The three areas you should evaluate are as follows:

- What are the school's strengths and weaknesses?
- What do you need help with and what do you already know?
- Do you need support through the process or are you happy to go it alone?

The key is to think about the school as a whole and not just your own expertise. As the project leader, it is likely that you will already possess a strong understanding of pedagogy and have a passion or experience with using technology for learning. Can the same be said about the rest of your school's teachers however? I have seen many schools whose project leader has blazed a trail that no one else could follow.

At an Apple event in the summer of 2015, I met a collection of teachers whose ICT leader was one of the most sought after iPad trainers in the UK. I mistakenly assumed that they would be comfortable and confident iPad users themselves as they work with this ICT leader every week. Imagine my surprise to find these teachers could barely use their iPads for little more than web browsing! All three teachers had been at the school for over four years, and while the ICT leader in question was using his iPad for great things, he had not invested the time to develop his own school as he should have done as project leader. This is why it is so important to have an iPad strategic team in place, because one person, regardless of their talents, is rarely enough to make a successful project.

With that in mind think about whether there is any help that the sales company may be able to offer to support the goal of developing a strategic team.

## INCLUDING YOUR FINANCE TEAM

A vital aspect of any large project is your finance team. It is important that you include them early in the project because you may not have full authority on purchasing decisions. The danger is that a company/salesperson works closely with the you through the proposal stage, developing a solution that is great for the school, only for the finance team to take over and select another cheaper supplier. Ultimately, you get what you pay for, and it should not surprise anyone that the company who offers the lowest price rarely provides the best service. More often you never hear from them again until it is time to buy something else. In the industry this is called *box shifting* and it is what has come to give salespeople such a bad name. One way to avoid this is to make sure your finance team is involved in the project from the outset so that they understand what you are trying to achieve.

## KEY TAKEAWAYS

- Think about your school's strengths and weaknesses, and find a supplier who can support these.

- Define what value is to your school. If you have the internal expertise and team to go it alone, then by all means look for the lowest price. However, if you do not then look for support and experience. You get what you pay for in life and you should not be surprised to know that the cheapest companies often offer the least after sales support.

- Question what any non ASE company brings to the table. You will likely already be paying more buying through them, and they also do not have access to Apple Education's wealth of support, best practice and resource.

## Chapter 9

# LEARNING TO TENDER

Learning to tender is a skill all schools should become familiar with. Setting out your requirements in a binding contract ensures that suppliers must give full transparency in their bids.

It is fair to say that most schools are not familiar with the tendering procedure. Historically, the majority of technology projects where either government funded (such as server installations) or straightforward hardware and installation jobs (such as computer suites). iPad projects, however, are much more complex, and having the ability to tender in your arsenal can save time, money and stress.

The tendering process has four parts to it, which I talk about in more detail below Figure A:

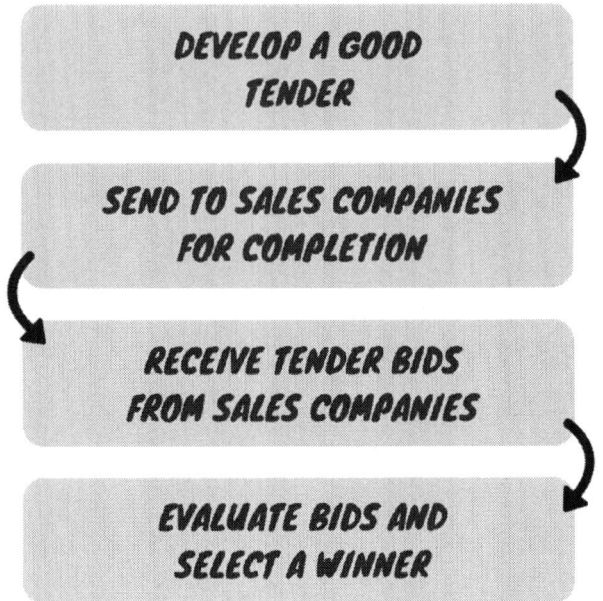

Figure A: Tender Process

## STAGE ONE: DEVELOPING A GOOD TENDER

A good tender always has the following three components:

- A specification of all products, support and value add you require
- Specific deadlines and deliverable timescales
- A scoring matrix to select a winning supplier bias free

This stage is work-intensive and requires the most careful preparation. I will break it down further to look at what is involved.

1. **Writing the specification**

A full tender often includes the following sections:

- **Tender Administration:** Your contact details, name of the school, deadlines and delivery timescales

- **Supplier Assessment Questionnaire (optional in this case):** Do potential suppliers need accreditations or certain qualifications to supply your school? This can be relevant on capital build projects or anything funded by the Education Funding Agency. Do you want to work with an organisation that has certain policies (Investor in People, Green Policy, etc.)?

- **Scope and Objectives:** What is your project and what are its aims? This is key to enabling potential suppliers to tailor their expertise to your requirements.

- **Statement of Requirements:** A list of the equipment and services your project requires

- **Escalation:** Who do you speak to at the supplier if something goes wrong or your first contact is away / unable to help?

- **Pricing proposal:** The list of equipment you specified in the Statement of Requirements along with submitted pricing.

- **Insurance (optional):** The terms and conditions of any insurance or warranties that the supplier may be offering.

- **Invoicing**: The payment and invoicing terms you require from the supplier. The standard is 30 days credit.

- **Contractual Terms and Conditions:** This is the legal element of the tender that outlines each party's responsibilities.

If you search Google for 'hardware tender template' you will get a number of pre-made templates that you can develop yours from. Just remember to change all the relevant details!

There is a lot to think about when writing your specification, so I have included some easy-to-follow tips to help you through the process.

**TIP#1: Do your research**, because you will need to write a specification for the hardware and services you require. Take the opportunity to visit schools who use iPads and speak to as many educators as you can who have experience on similar projects. Use Twitter to join networks with educators worldwide and gain a wealth of advice and information. Look for school projects that inspire you and see if the people involved have a Twitter presence. Post questions and use relevant hashtags. The following should help you meet the right people:

- #edtech
- #iPadEd
- #mlearning
- #ukedchat
- #aussieEd

**TIP#2: Do not rely on salespeople for advice.** Manufacturers incentivise companies with better margins if they sell more of their product, so sales companies select a number of preferred options and create a vendor list. If you invite a company to meet for their advice, you are already on the back foot. Proposals will vary from company to company, but the reality is that it is all biased information. They promote what they make the most money on. This is most common on MDMs, backend storage solutions and hardware accessories such as cases.

**TIP#3: Go direct to the manufacture for trial software.** The majority of manufacturers (MDM and storage solutions in particular) will happily supply you with software to test. Do specify that you do not wish your details to be passed onto sales companies at this stage however, because software manufacturers rarely sell direct and will quickly handover your details to their partners if they sense a sale on the horizon.

**TIP#4: Consider buying direct from insurance and leasing companies.** Margins are negotiated on a company-by-company basis, but a sales company will normally make a mark-up of 10-20% on insurance and 2-5% on a lease. This can easily mount up to tens of thousands of pounds on large scale projects. To get you started, I have listed a few of the key players in the education market that I have worked with in the past. I do not personally endorse any of the companies below; I will leave it to you to decide who is right for your project.

| Lease providers | Insurance provider |
|---|---|
| Apple Financial Services | Burnett Insurance (part of SPB group) |
| CHG Meridian | Endsleigh |
| CPU Group | Summit Insurance Services Ltd |

| Econocom |  |
|---|---|
| GE Capital |  |

Bear in mind that you will need to have a completed supplier tender before you can speak to a lease provider, as they will need to know the amount that you want to finance.

**TIP#5: Include delivery deadlines and a margin protection clause in your tender.** This will protect your school from actions beyond your or your supplier's control. When Apple releases a new model of iPad, the previous model usually drops in price. The reduction can be as much as 20%. If this happens, you want to ensure the school is the beneficiary of the savings, not the sales company.

To write a margin protection clause, include a paragraph that requires the supplier to disclose their margin on the price stated in their tender. Then, state that if there are any price reductions to your chosen model of iPad over a set time frame (usually six months), the supplier must honour to sell the new model at the agreed margin. New iPad models typical launch in the autumn. If you tender in the summer for delivery in September, this can make a margin protection clause a very worthwhile inclusion in your tender.

## 2. Creating a scoring matrix

A scoring matrix is the backbone to a good tender, and it should help you pick your supplier without bias. The matrix is made up of the key points for your project, which you allocate a scoring weight to. Your scoring matrix should always be included in your tender to suppliers, allowing them to tailor their response to your needs.

A typical education tender will include the following aspects and I would recommend following this structure:

| Section | Scoring |
| --- | --- |
| Price | 70% |
| Specification | 20% |
| Value Add | 10% |
| Optionals (such as environmental policy) | |

The **specification** is deemed as the accuracy of the products and services a company includes in their submission to what you have specified. This may sound like common sense, but you would not believe how many times a sales company will switch out a product you have specified for something different.

This can be a *'foot in the door'* strategy, offering you a different product from your request along with an invitation to come out and personally discuss it with you. Transparency runs both ways in a tender process, so if you meet with one sales company you should agree to meet with all. This becomes very time consuming, and all because the companies could not meet your request for a certain product! When the specification is weighted however, only the naive sales companies will try and substitute the products you specify.

**TIP#6: Have a higher score weighting towards value-add.**
Value add is what a supplier can do for you beyond the equipment you buy and the price they charge. If you increase the weighting of

the value-add component you can often receive heavily discounted or in some cases free installation, setup and support. You may be offered a larger allocation of training. The supplier may offer to make you a case study site, or host a future networking event in your school. Depending on the company, the offers vary widely.

I believe that value add is important for schools because implementation is key on large technology projects. iPads are generally sold at between 3-6% mark-up, so if you only prioritise getting the lowest price, your savings will equate to a few pound per device. Implementation is often a school's biggest weakness, both on the technical side in getting iPads up and running, and on the pedagogical side, ensuring they are embedded into the learning. This is simply because schools have never needed these two skills until recently, making it unlikely that they will already be in-house.

**TIP#7: Send your tender out to a range of suppliers.** Do not just pick the cheapest companies in the marketplace. Include companies known for their training and support to ensure you get plenty of options for your project that are not just based on cost.

## STAGE TWO: INVITING COMPANIES TO TENDER

With your tender written, it is time to send it out. You will be able to find suppliers using the Apple Solution Expert (ASE) locator on Apple's education website.

Remember that the locator only returns ASEs within a certain radius to your location and does not take into account any regional or secondary offices a company may have. To get a full national listing of ASEs, run the search a few times using the main cities across England. This will pull up each company's contact details and website address. Almost all ASEs have a generic sales@ email address, so emailing your tender to that should be enough to start the process.

Any reputable sales company will request to organise a meeting to better understand your requirements for the tender. It is worthwhile taking the time to agree to these, because not all ASEs will supply the same solution and the meeting will be your opportunity to quiz them on what they can and cannot do. Schedule a day in the diary and allocate meeting slots to each company.

## STAGE THREE: RECEIVING TENDER BIDS FROM SALES COMPANIES

You should schedule 7-14 days to review all the bids you receive, as this process always takes longer than you may imagine. Make sure you leave enough time between announcing the tender and the deadline for delivery to enable you to receive, score and select a winner.

## STAGE FOUR: SCORING THE RESPONSES

Once you have received the final submissions, it is time to get scoring. I have seen some very complex formulas for scoring tenders at college level and above. Some were so complex that I wondered whether the maths department had banded together in a bid to stage a coup! I propose keeping it simple and working out scores with some good old-fashioned tools: a pen, piece of paper and a calculator.

First, assemble a panel to judge the tender bids. It is helpful to have a range of perspectives represented here, so include staff from the early adopters, majority, and laggard camps as well as staff from across the school authority scale. It is also useful to have an odd number of people on the scoring panel as this will greatly reduce the likelihood of getting a tie between submissions.

Your scoring system should already be in place from when you created your scoring matrix. You need to stick to the weightings you have sent out.

When the time comes to start marking the bids, every member of the panel should mark free from influence. It is perfectly fine to discuss the options on the table, but think of the marking process like voting. Each panel member will need to compare all submissions across each section (pricing, specification, value add, anything else) and score it competitively. The maximum points per category will be 10, so the company offering the best or most competitive response in each section will receive 10 points, the second best scores 9 points, and so on.

The overall winner is calculated by collating members' individual scores and taking the average in each category. This will ensure impartiality. Let us look at the table. In this example, a panel of five teachers are judging tenders from three companies: Tablet Genius*, ThinkSmart* and IT Solutions*. The table shows their individual scores for each company.

The final score for the category is calculated by multiplying the average score by the weighted scoring percentage, in this case, 70%.

| Supplier / Respondent | Tablet Genius | Think Smart | IT Solutions |
|---|---|---|---|
| John | 10 | 9 | 8 |
| Sarah | 9 | 10 | 8 |
| Mo | 9 | 10 | 8 |
| Remi | 10 | 9 | 8 |
| Romesh | 10 | 8 | 9 |
| Average | 9.6 | 8.8 | 8.2 |

Weighting percentage: 70%

Tablet Genius     9.6 x 0.7 = 6.7
ThinkSmart        8.8 x 0.7 = 6.2
IT Solutions      8.2 x 0.7 = 5.7

**Final score for Pricing section:**

**Tablet Genius = 6.7**
**ThinkSmart = 6.2**
**IT Solutions = 5.7**

Use this method to calculate the winner for each section, add each section's score together and the company with the highest total is your winner!

## TENDER & PROCUREMENT PORTALS

If you put your project to tender, you have the option of using a tender portal. These portals allow schools to post tender requirements online, and for sales companies to access them and submit bids. Plenty of portals exist because they can be very lucrative businesses. The advantage of using a portal is that it brings a large number of suppliers together quickly and easily.

In my experience, however, there are a number of drawbacks, and you need to ask yourself whether you want to put your school at risk of these. There is very little inspection of this industry, which means anything can go. Some portal providers require potential suppliers to pay a *'marketing fee'*, which is little more than an entrance charge before they can access the system. The fee is often substantial too; I know of a portal run by an independent school in the North of England who require companies to make a £2000 *'marketing'* payment to register on their system! Fees like this drive away smaller, local and often more value-add focused suppliers.

You might also be put off by the fact that portal providers take a 1-2% commission fee from the winning bid. That cost is factored into the selling price to you, meaning you pay more than you would have done going direct to the supplier.

Portals tend to be used for bigger, more lucrative contracts, and herein lies the biggest danger for your school: portals' reputation attracts companies who are looking for the chance for large profit margins and are non-too-concerned about whether your project has any impact on learning at all. I think the following story best demonstrates how quickly things can fall apart when the wrong sales company ends up on your school's doorstep:

### Case Study: Greenacre*

*Greenacre Independent\* had a vision of a three-year transition to a full mobile learning environment, and decided to put their project to tender through a portal. I had worked with this school in the past, but the company I worked for at the time was not registered on this particular portal system as it required a substantial 'marketing' fee to join, so I bowed out of the process. Their project leader David\* kept me abreast of developments after the deployment.*

*He told me that on the first day of the autumn term, five hundred iPads and cases turned up at the school in a DHL van. The school received no advanced notification from the supplier of their arrival, and there were no employees from the supplier onsite to support them. Greenacre only had one full-time IT technician, who had no previous technical knowledge on Apple products. The school had invested their whole budget into hardware, so there was no money left for after sales support. As a result, they were unable to deploy apps, manage the devices or even get them working consistently on the WiFi. This continued throughout the first year and by the second summer, the school's governing body was so alarmed at the deployment's failure that they decided to kill the project. They had invested well over £200,000 up to that point.*

The winning company for the Greenacre bid was not a certified ASE; in fact, none of the suppliers who bid through the portal were. Whichever supplier Greenacre had chosen, they would not have had access to the quality of support they needed to get the project up and running. Ironically, by using a tender portal, they siphoned off many of the ASEs who could have made their project a success, instead attracting a company without expertise and interested only in profit.

It is logical to steer clear of private run portals, either by a school or by a company. This leaves government portals and agreements, which would appear to be fully above board. These often run in a specific geographical location (although any school is free to purchase through them provided they operate under the same education system). The government (either local or national) tender upfront by creating a 'shopping list' of the most popular technology that schools are buying. A contract is then awarded to a winning supplier and schools have a set buying price.

Sounds perfect you may think, but these also have pitfalls to be aware of. Another 'trick of the trade' that companies use in these types of arrangement is strategic pricing. This is when a company quotes a very low price on the current iPad to win the procurement contract, in the knowledge that the new model of Pad is soon to be launched. Upon its release, the company can raise its prices to whatever it likes. If a government or council has already signed a procurement agreement, often schools are legally bound to it and must pay the higher price. There is a country in Europe who tender a three year iPad contract that locks schools into a single supplier. This hands the sales company a monopoly and they use strategic pricing to make millions from it.

## KEY TAKEAWAYS

- Take the procurement process seriously. If you are spending vast sums of money on your project, then think about tendering. Not only does this alleviate the back-and-forth between sales companies and your school, but it also gives you a framework to score your potential suppliers on more than just price alone.

- Do your research before getting quotes. You need to know what you are buying to ensure you get the most competitive pricing.

- If you are taking delivery at a later date think about writing in a margin protection clause to protect against future price changes to ensure you get the benefit of any price reductions.

# THE TABLET REVOLUTION

## Chapter 10

# FINANCING

Putting a financial plan in place is vital. Schools often enter into iPad projects without any clear long-term plan of action for funding, and simply buy as many devices as they can afford each year; thirty one year, sixty the next, and so on. Over time this accumulates to significant amounts of money, all without any clear plan of action. It is my view that this manner of purchasing blunts the impact of the iPad and is the reason why mobile technology has proved largely ineffective in education so far. The 2015 OECD study *'Students, Computers and Learning'* found that even countries that have invested heavily in information and communication technologies (ICT) for education have seen no noticeable improvement in their performances in PISA results for reading, mathematics or science.

It is clear that a new approach is needed in schools over the current one of stockpiling technology. Buying enough iPads outright for every student is unattainable for all but a handful of schools, which is all the more reason to undertake some long-term financial planning. An easy figure to remember is that for every 100 students, it costs roughly £20,000 to buy them each an iPad Mini with a case. However, that does not take into account any infrastructure upgrades that you may need, which can add up to tens of thousands. This *'buy it outright'* strategy is not working in the UK and is unsustainable. So, other than raiding the staff room sofas for loose change, what **is** the right way to fund your project?

## EXPLORING THE FUNDING OPTIONS

You have two options to fund your iPad project: **payment upfront** or payment over a set term (known as **leasing**). Many schools write off their ability to undertake an iPad project because they do not have the money to buy the number of devices they want. Instead, they buy small batches of 30-50 devices when they can. This works for a pilot scheme, but if you are committed to developing mobile technology for learning, continuing to buy iPads outright is a bad plan. It is expensive and gives you minimal availability throughout the school. This more than anything, blunts the effectiveness the iPad can have.

The majority of schools who undertake large 1:1 iPad projects lease their devices. I want you to consider this for your own project. Leasing is beneficial as it increases the amount of equipment you can afford, fixes outgoings over a set period, and enables you to implement a refresh plan for when the technology needs to be replaced. Before you take this to the powers that be at your own school, it is important to know that leasing is still a tarnished word for many in education. Through the 90s and early 00s, a lot of schools were ripped off by companies supplying printers and network hardware at astronomical interest rates over lengthy contracts. Things have thankfully improved significantly since then, with better regulation and plenty of competition in the market to ensure you can shop around for the best rates. Leasing is again a reliable funding option that should be given consideration. Let me give you a brief overview of how it works for a school.

## LEASING

An **operational lease** is an agreement to rent hardware over a fixed term before returning it. It is the only kind of lease available to schools, and means you do not have ownership of the hardware. This is important to factor into your financial planning as it can make a huge difference to the impact of your project. Schools traditionally look to stockpile resources, but this is not a good idea if your resources are iPads. Tablets have a lower lifespan than computers, and while many schools get eight years out of desktop computers, you are likely to only see half that lifespan with iPads. The other issue is the rate of change from apps on the iPad. Each year, Apple releases a new iPad operating system (called iOS) and app-makers rush to update their app to take advantage of the new operating system. In many instances, there is little backwards compatibility, meaning that if you do not upgrade the iOS on your iPads you cannot download that app.

Some schools decide not to update their iPads in order to maximise their lifespan, but this can create more problems than it solves. When new versions of apps are released, work created in those apps is not always compatible with previous versions. This means that if you get new iPads in the future, the work created on them may not open on your older iPads, unless you have kept the software and apps up to date. This creates a serious workflow problem in the classroom.

Financing your iPad rollout through an operating lease allows you to avoid these headaches. It also means you can develop your project beyond the next 12 months. It gives you definite costs that you can plan into the long-term budgets. When you lease equipment over 3 years, it costs about 90% of its full value. To lease 800 iPads would cost in total around £135,000 rather than the £150,000 needed to buy them outright. That is a significant saving, but the thing that is more impactful is the immediate access to technology you get with leasing. Compare the tablet where a school is spending the same amount each year on the project:

|      | Leasing          |              | Outright Purchase |                        |
|------|------------------|--------------|-------------------|------------------------|
| Year | iPads available  | Leasing Cost | iPads available   | Outright Purchase Cost |
| 1    | 800              | £45,000      | 267               | £50,000                |
| 2    | 800              | £45,000      | 534               | £50,000                |
| 3    | 800              | £45,000      | 800               | £50,000                |

If you are put-off by the idea that leasing is a continued on-going cost, you should be prepared for the reality that there are always on-going costs to running iPad schemes. It is not so much a case of how to avoid costs, as how to get the most out of what you *do* spend.

## BENEFITS OF LEASING

**Ubiquitous access to technology**

By leasing equipment you get instant access to all the technology you need on day one. This is important, because it allows the school learning environment to evolve quicker. If every student has access to a device, teachers and departments can take advantage of that straightaway.

**No incompatibility**

Leases are agreed over set periods, usually 3 year terms, and at the end of that agreement all iPads will be returned and new devices will be issued as the lease starts fresh. This is beneficial as it ensure there are no legacy (old) devices within the school that may have become obsolete. This keeps workflow in perfect order and reduces major headaches for students and teachers.

**Fixed costs**

Apple could change their pricing structure at any time or they may kill their entry level model. That means that even if you budget to buy the iPads outright next year, when the time comes you may find you no longer have enough money. By leasing your devices you have a fixed annual cost that can be accommodated into the school budget.

There are many benefits to leasing, but I am not proposing that you should begin leasing masses of iPads tomorrow for your school; I am actually proposing a more strategic evaluation of your school's purchasing habits. Do not buy iPads outright in batches each year without a long-term plan, because it is unlikely to give you any benefit. The fact is an iPad project is always an on-going cost whether you buy devices outright or lease them, so before you embark think carefully about the long term financial plan. Is your school is able to invest in the technology consistently to a level that it will benefit from?

## PARENTAL CONTRIBUTION SCHEMES

An increasingly popular method to mitigate the limitations of your school budget is to supplement the project costs with parental contributions. In its most basic form, parents pay monthly for their child to have use of an iPad while in school. Typically, but not always, the device becomes the property of the parent at the end of the agreed term. Developing a successful parental contribution scheme requires detailed planning and coordination from the school's leadership team, along with an open dialogue with parents throughout.

The basic mechanics of a parental contribution scheme are as follows:

### Source Costs
Source hardware cost from supplier. Open dialogue with parents and gauge interest.

### Open Portal
Hardware supplier creates scheme portal. Parents sign up to a direct debit agreement for repayments.

### Place Orders
Place orders. Supplier arranges lease on school's behalf.

### Sign Lease
School underwrites the lease, agreeing to quarterly repayments and financial responsibility.

### Repayments Collected
Repayments usually collected a month in advance from parents before devices are delivered.

### End of Lease
On the completion of the lease, parents have the option to take ownership of the device, or return it to the lease provider and enrol into another scheme.

There are 4 stakeholders in a parental contribution scheme:

- the school
- the parent

- the hardware supplier
- the lease company

That is a simple explanation of what can be complex arrangement. There are several key aspects you need to consider to ensure your scheme runs smoothly:

**A watertight vision for the project:** If you embark on a parental contribution scheme, you will be asking parents to pay for a learning resource out of their own pocket. This will grate with anyone who is less than convinced of its benefits. Prepare for a grilling at project open evenings, and have a clearly defined vision. This should include project benchmarks that you can share with parents: what are the goals for this project at the end of year one, two and three, and how will this improve learning? In the best case scenario, you may get 70% signup from parents in year one, but I have seen schools run schemes with as little as 30% uptake. Your vision should include the minimum number of devices you will need per classroom because you cannot improve learning if access for students is poor.

**Contributions towards repayments from the school:** Schools should always contribute to the repayments of these devices regardless of whether parents take ownership at the end of the agreement or not. This project is your bid to improve the school's learning environment: it is not a cost-saving exercise. If your school chooses not to contribute, you open yourself up to criticism: why should parents fork out if the school is not willing to? The unspoken rule is that the school should pick up the VAT costs of the scheme. Doing so can greatly reduce the price of the scheme against the high street cost for parents and this should incentivise more to sign up.

**Use of additional monetary support:** Used properly, iPads can narrow the gap just as well as any other learning intervention for underperforming students. If those students receive additional financial support in the form of Pupil Premium or something else, use as much as possible to offset the cost of the devices for those students and parents.

**Understanding your financial responsibility:** It continues to surprise me that HMRC or the Department of Education have not issued some information surrounding parental contribution schemes. The financial buck stops with the school on these schemes no matter how you arrange them. It is **always** the school that underwrites the lease. If parents decide to stop paying before the agreement ends, the legal responsibility is on the school to make up any shortfall. Typically schools do not budget for this eventuality, so it represents a financial risk if parents decide they no longer want to keep up repayments. A school has no legal recourse should parents stop repayments, because you need a Consumer Credit License to create a legally binding contract for extended payment terms. Parents are signing a direct debit agreement with the hardware solution provider to administer the repayments, but at the time of writing this, not one provider has a Consumer Credit License giving them no power beyond your own. Be clear on the financing before launching any parental contribution scheme.

**GAP insurance** covers the amount on the lease that is the difference between the asset value and the repayment total. The asset value of a product is based on its depreciation, but products do not depreciate in a consistent manner. When you sign up to a lease you agree a set monthly payment, but often over the first year you will pay less than the depreciation of the product's asset value. Imagine you lease an iPad and your repayments over the first year total £90, but the iPad's value has dropped £100. If you were to stop paying the lease provider will have made a £10 loss. This occurs for two reasons. First because people want newer products and will pay more for them, and second because of VAT (sales tax for those outside of the UK). In the second and third years the rate of depreciation slows and repayments catch up and overtake the asset value of the product. In a school context this means that if parents sign up but then stop paying early, there is a shortfall in repayments that the school is responsible for covering. By including GAP insurance into the arrangement it removes this risk completely, but it will increase the repayment costs for each parent. It is a balancing act as you do not want to price parents out, but you want to cover yourself. In my career I have only met a single school that has become unstuck because of parents' refusal to make payments. The more likely issue is that children leave the school or a family's financial circumstances change (loss of a job), so it is good to pre-empt these issues and plan for them. One thing that has popped up over the last few years is that sales companies create a 'rainy day fund' for a school to draw upon should they run into an unexpected financial hurdle. This fund is usually created by charging all parents a nominal extra such as 50p on their monthly repayment. Parents are rarely told about this upfront as it creates a difficult situation. You are asking the majority to pay insurance to cover the potential actions of a minority. This never goes down well! I favour making GAP insurance mandatory for all or having the school put aside a lump sum in case of an emergency.

It may look like parental contribution schemes are more trouble than they are worth but the key is to simply understand the legal responsibilities of everyone involved so that your scheme is prepared for all eventualities. If you do that then it should be a success.

## BRING YOUR OWN DEVICE (BYOD)

If families already own a device, you may find that parents prefer their child to bring it rather than signing up to buy another. This is called 'Bring Your Own Device' and offers a school the option to flood classrooms with the latest technology without the financial outlay associated with doing so. It almost sounds too good to be true, and it pretty much is for all but a handful of schools. Opting for BYOD can be troublesome, and I would recommend exercising great caution if you decide to go down this route. There are several issues that you will need to give a lot of thought to before committing to a BYOD scheme:

**The difficulty of mixed-platform BYOD:** Mixed-platform BYOD (Apple, Android & Windows) is, from a technical standpoint, a challenge beyond the skill set of most schools due to the software costs and personnel skills required. It is also pedagogically unsustainable for teaching staff. Apps are not always available cross-platform, so lesson planning is difficult if multiple devices need to be used. Powerful education content platforms, such as iTunes U and iBooks, are Apple only, and there are no ready-made alternatives on Android or Microsoft devices. This makes it difficult to develop learning that will use devices beyond research or web browsing. One way to pre-empt this situation is to lay down clear guidelines about which devices and models your BYOD scheme is open to, a limitation, which might prove unpopular with parents who own a device that is not on the approved list.

**Keeping students safe online:** Parents who own a device are often willing to allow their child to take it to school. This is a non-starter, because it opens the door for inappropriate content to be accessed by children. I am not necessarily referring to X-rated websites; in fact, it is usually social media sites that are to blame, because most do not age-check content. In 2015, Facebook was surrounded by controversy over a video of graphic hostage executions by terrorists that autoplayed on its newsfeed; the same year, Instagram faced complaints over semi-nude photographs posted by users with the hashtag 'EDM' (relating to electronic dance music festivals).

Cloud syncing, which is becoming more popular with app developers is another issue for schools. For example, Apple's iCloud function will automatically sync any photo saved to the camera roll across all devices associated with that Apple ID. This is an issue I have seen first hand when a child brought their mother's iPad into school, unaware that it was syncing photos. Throughout the day, inappropriate content populated on the iPad originating from the mother's iPhone. If a child shows their friends 18+ content on their parent's iPad during school time, you have a major e-safety issues on your hands. If you run a BYOD scheme stipulate that the device must be the student's own, and not a family or shared device.

**The educational cost of sharing devices with the family:** The very idea that a tool for learning must be shared with the family for generic use is problematic, in my view. It is not ideal that students should have to return their device to someone else once they get home. I know of BYOD schemes that have suffered for this very reason. A high-achieving student in one school I worked with began to fall behind with her work after the school implemented iPad-orientated homework. Why? It turned out that each night her grandmother, who owned the iPad, used it to play online bingo until the small hours, allowing no time for the girl to complete her homework. The scheme's use of family devices threw the principle of 24/7 access to learning right out of the window.

## GIFT AID

When parental contribution portals first sprung up across the country, a number used Gift Aid to supplement the costs of their schemes. Charities on a mission to close the 'digital divide' became involved with parental contribution schemes, offering to administer the repayments and to apply Gift Aid on donations, effectively reducing hardware costs by 25%.

At the time this became popular, I was running the Northern territory for a big Apple reseller and was working on a number of large 1:1 projects. From the outset, I understood that Gift Aid could not be legally claimed by schools, and made the decision to avoid working with these charities on any of our schemes.

Our company could not match a charity's offer of 25% off hardware costs, and we lost bids to them every time. Nevertheless, we did not sway from our ethics because I understood the consequences. In early 2014, one of this charity's flagship 1:1 projects eventually fell foul of the law when HMRC looked at the scheme and judged Gift Aid was not applicable. The scheme funding fell short by tens of thousands, which the school were then responsible for because they underwrote the lease. This scandal never made headline news, but it did go some way to reduce the influence of these types of charities. The most troubling news for schools who have already opted for Gift Aid is that HMRC can backdate payments for years ahead, meaning they would be liable should their finances ever come under scrutiny.

HMRC and the Department of Education have since updated their documents for Gift Aid on schools purchases, and now offer clear and straightforward guidance. The full document can be found on the gov.uk site, but there are only three factors that you need to take into account. You cannot claim Gift Aid on:

- Any payment relating to goods or services
- Gifts that come with a condition about repayment
- A 'minimum donation' where there is no choice about payment

No matter how you arrange your scheme, repayments or anything else, Gift Aid is not applicable to iPad schemes.

## KEY TAKEAWAYS

- iPads are not like other school resources. You cannot stockpile them the way you can with calculators or scissors, so plan a refresh cycle from the beginning to give you a deployment timeline. Going into a project with the intention to 'buy as many as you can' each year is a recipe for little impact.

- Do not write leasing off before you have given it some attention. My opinion is that all schools should lease their ICT because it maximises availability to students while minimising yearly costs. You can lease three times more equipment than you can buy outright. Think about the cost of having two thirds of students without access to a iPad in the first year. What learning opportunities are you losing in that scenario?

- Engage parents early and frequently on parental contribution schemes, and understand that the financial buck stops with the school. These schemes can be a serious money maker for salespeople, and less reputable ones will say whatever you want to hear to move the process forward. Unless the school or the sales company collecting the repayments has a consumer credit license, you have little legal recourse or leverage should a parent decide to jump out of the scheme midway through.

# Chapter 11

# BEYOND THE SCHOOL GATE

There are few things more powerful in a child's education than an engaged parent. In the UK, the Department for Children, School and Families found that for children up to age 11, parental engagement had a bigger impact on student performance than the quality of the school. How you engage with students outside of school can be every bit as important as what you do in the classroom, so it is vital that your iPad project reflects this.

ESSA Academy, arguably one of the world's most successful iPad schools attribute their success to what they have termed *'the ability to expand time.'* For students at ESSA, learning does not stop at the school gate; it stretches to anywhere they wish. Every department has developed its own bespoke resources so that students are able to access all of their course materials at home. Providing their students with learning materials has enabled parents to take a bigger role in their child's education and this is one of the factors in how ESSA have transformed so significantly: since 2009 the academy has improved their 5 A*- C GCSE pass rate from 63% to 99%.

## HOW TO BRIDGE THE GAP

If you only use iPads in lessons, then your model of engagement looks something like this:

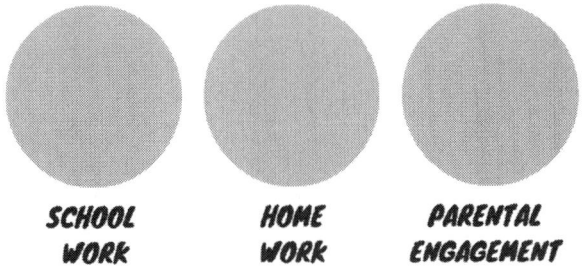

Each element in this traditional engagement model is separated from the other with little overlap.

Allowing the iPad to go home creates a new model of engagement that bridges the gap between each and can maximise the impact of your project on learning. It looks something like this:

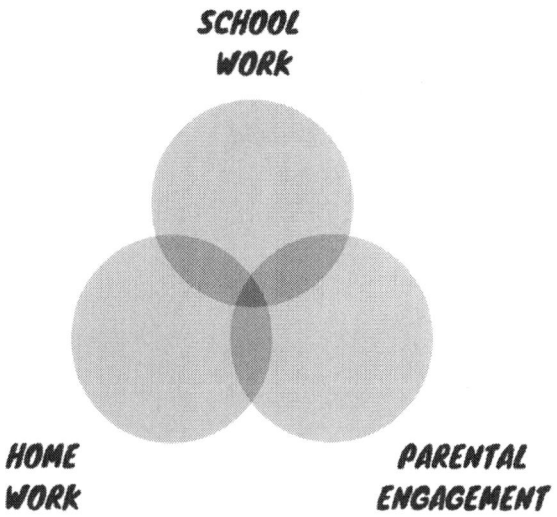

**SCHOOL WORK**

**HOME WORK**

**PARENTAL ENGAGEMENT**

In this model parents are kept abreast of what happens in school because they are able to see it in action at home.

Let us look at this in more detail.

## COURSE MATERIAL AVAILABLE AT HOME

Independent learning is one of education's hottest topics at the moment, but so long as students are reliant on teachers to deliver a subject's curriculum, true independent learning will remain nothing more than a pipe dream. Apple offer two very powerful and completely free platforms that enable you to package the curriculum up and deliver it to students at their own pace. These are iBooks and iTunes U.

iBooks allows you to create digital books, complete with videos, photographs, audio clips and many other interactive elements, while iTunes U is a MOOC (Massive Open Online Course) that enables you to upload and deliver a series of lessons, lectures or seminars for students to digest at their own pace. Both of these platforms enable the school to begin implementing *blended learning*. When students can access lesson material ahead of time, they are able to read ahead and bring their understanding to the lesson. Whether the students were really able to understand the material or not, it still aids the progression of learning because teachers are spending less time imparting knowledge and more time developing it. If a student reads at home for the upcoming algebra module but does not understand it, when the student comes to class the teacher can ask **what** it is they do not fully understand and spend time on that. The result is that lessons require less demonstration, with more time for discussion and coaching.

## PARENTAL ENGAGEMENT EVENINGS

Parents will have a lot of questions about your project once they are on board, so be prepared. Do not be surprised if you are met with scepticism in the early stages: *'My child already spends all day staring at smartphone and tablet screens like a zombie. How could an iPad possibly help their learning?'* The key to engaging parents is to get them involved as soon as possible in the form of a parental engagement evening, and to make the aims and outcomes of your project known. Most parents are unlikely to understand the educational benefits of iPads until you explain them, so speak about the impact you envisage, and be clear and specific. They will see through waffle.

In my experience, there are six main areas of contention for parents when it comes to iPad deployments:

1. The parental contribution scheme is too expensive
2. It is a waste of money - the impact does not justify the cost
3. I never had an iPad in school and I did alright!
4. iPads will make lessons worse because they will distract the class
5. My child might access adult content through a school iPad
6. I do not want my child walking around with an iPad because it leaves them at greater risk of getting mugged

Your project vision should already cover answering the first four of these points, and the school's Acceptable User Policy (AUP) will reassure them regarding the issue of e-safety and inappropriate content.

This leaves the final objection: personal safety. Some parents worry that unsavoury individuals will line up outside the school, demanding students hand over their iPad once school lets out. There are a number of ways to dispel this worry. First speak to other iPad schools and get their story. On all the projects I have worked, including those in the toughest inner city schools, I am yet to hear of any thefts or muggings taking place outside of school. Secondly, if it is a concern at your location then speak with your local police station, or better yet invite a police spokesperson to tackle this question head on at the parents evening. Often the police are more than happy to send in a PCO to the school. The police are targeted with outreach work, as prevention is always better than reaction. Inviting the police in can build a valuable relationship that can keep children safe, educate pupils and reduce future youth crime. Finally if those first two do not work simply apply common sense. Most children already have a smartphone, iPod, camera or other device worth hundreds of pounds on them. Students are not mugged for these on a production line scale after school, so it is highly unlikely they will be for an iPad.

I want to demonstrate the difference proper planning can make to parental engagement evenings with the following two case studies. As you can see for these schools, their parental engagement was the difference between success and failure:

### Case Study: Lowacre High School*

*Lowacre High School* is located in a deprived area of Blackpool. They wanted to launch a parental contribution scheme that would enable students to get their own iPads. Unfortunately, the headteacher saw the project as a cost saving exercise more than a tool to improve learning, and tried to put it upon parents to fully fund it. Usually, schools contribute financially to these type of schemes, either picking up the VAT costs or using Pupil Premium funding to offset costs, but this school did neither. On the night of their parental engagement evening, they gathered over 300 parents into the hall to launch their vision of equipping every child with a iPad. Questions came thick and fast from parents, but the staff were unable to offer any insight or clarity into why the project should go ahead and how the cost to parents was justified. With no answers forthcoming, the discontent in the room soon turned to anger and choice words were thrown across the room towards the staff. The headteacher made a quick bee-line for the door and the evening was abandoned. The school went back to the drawing board and took their time to flesh out their vision, and organised a second launch evening. This time less than fifty parents turned up and only a handful signed up to the iPad scheme. When the signup period for the scheme closed, from two year groups with over 500 children, only sixty parents had signed up for an iPad. In the end, the scheme was completely abandoned.*

## Case Study: Abbot Beyne

*When I worked with Abbot Beyne School they bucked the trend and allowed students to take home an iPad despite the school funding the project. However they did so with one caveat. Parents had to attend a 45 minute evening meeting, before their child was allowed to take an iPad home. At this meeting the school gave a detailed presentation of their vision for the future of learning at Abbot Beyne, sharing and bringing parents into the fold. Abbot Beyne then made parents active members of the iPad project by requiring them to read and sign an Acceptable User Policy (AUP) with their son or daughter. This outlined the expectations of all parties on the project, so that parent, student and school each knew their responsibilities. It also offered parents the opportunity to talk with the school's project leader and raise any concerns or objections they may have. This sounds like a common sense approach, but it is surprising how few schools engage with parents to this extent. There is a big difference between telling parents and engaging them.*

*For Abbot Beyne School, parent evening attendance had plateaued at 60%. This figure may sound familiar: it is the national average in the UK. At the iPad launch evening, 198 out of 200 parents attended. The two that did not make it had already spoken to the school about their prior commitments and arranged a separate time later in the week. This was the first time the school had the opportunity to speak to many of their students' parents and it proved to be hugely beneficial. This level of parental engagement continued long after the students took their iPad home, and Abbot Beyne maintained a high 90% attendance rate for parents evenings throughout the rest of the school year. By engaging parents early in the project, the school made them active stakeholders in their child's education and they were able to see the work done in school on the iPad each night. Parental engagement is one of the most powerful factors in any child's achievement, and the interest that Abbot Beyne sparked on those launch evenings led to a deeper motivation in their students that is continuing to be reflected in the quality of work. Two years after launching their iPad project, the school received their highest ever GCSE performance.*

## KEY TAKEAWAYS

- What you do to support learning outside of school is just as important as what you do within school.

- Strong parental engagement sits at the core of all successful iPad projects. Engage early and be open and honest.

- Engaging parents goes right back to your vision and plan. Without these parents will see right through the project, any attempt to leverage them for funding will be unsuccessful.

# Chapter 12

# ENGAGING WITH SOCIAL MEDIA

## "WHAT DID YOU DO AT SCHOOL TODAY?"

You might recall being asked this question as a child, and answering it with varying degrees of detail depending on how much you wanted to go and play instead. Nevertheless, it is a moment of contact between parent and child, in which the parent shows their interest and tries to get some insight into their child's learning experience. Simple conversations like these can be crucial in nurturing a child's motivation in their own learning. If no one seems to care what they do at school, why should they?

A study into the lives and routines of 2000 British families, commissioned by Highland Spring in 2015 found that the 'average' family has just 34 minutes per evening together of undistracted time, without gadgets or distractions, where they feel they actually bond.

Longer working hours, lengthy commutes and stress are just some of the reasons underpinning the degradation of family time in Britain, but whatever the root cause, I believe that there are many ways schools can counteract this. Parental engagement is certainly one. Your aim is for parents to be interested in what their child does in school and for the child to be excited to share this with them. At the heart of parental engagement is the idea that your efforts will stir parents to ask, 'What did you do at school today?'

I believe that one of the strongest ways to reach out to parents is to embrace social media. It is free, time-efficient and can be used on a daily basis. Across the UK, around 40% of parents do not attend parent evenings either by choice or due to prior commitments, so it is time to start thinking outside of the box about how to engage this group.

When it comes to using social media in education, you have a choice of Facebook or Twitter. Facebook has more users, but their lack of restrictions on what people can post make it poorly suited in education. Twitter has a lot more educational uses, and its real-time stream design means it is much more engaging if you are live posting about field trips or school projects.

## Case Study: Tormead School

*James South, project leader at Tormead School, Guildford, commented to me that their social media output has been a contributing factor for prospective parents selecting their school over others. With teachers posting photos and short video examples of good work, science experiments, school trip blogs, and house singing, parents are able to get a real feel for the day to day life at Tormead far beyond what any glossy brochure would conjure up.*

## WHAT TO POST?

Embracing social media should have two clear goals: first, to engage parents with what is happening in classrooms. Second, to inspire and motivate students to produce their best work. Here are a few examples of what you can post:

| Class Update | School Update |
| --- | --- |
| **Motivation**: Excellent classwork from John… | **Save the Date**: 23rd March Parents Evening. Doors open at 7pm |
| **Discussion**: Who was the greatest American president? | **Exam Timetable**: GCSE maths starts 1pm tomorrow in the Hall |

| | |
|---|---|
| **Live Updates**: Here are our photos from Hadrian's Wall. Did you know it was built in... | **School Performances**: Don't forget, Alice in Wonderland production 24th April. Get tickets from Mrs Alsager |
| **Reminders**: Don't forget GCSE art projects are due tomorrow!! | **Celebrations**: Well done to all the Year 10s who passed their Duke of Edinburgh this weekend! |

The aim should be to make your posts a point of discussion between parent and child. Many primary schools have embraced Twitter and are leading by example in the UK education system. One of the best examples I have seen is from primary teacher who creates a *'Highlights from Today'* video displaying a few seconds of the selected pupil's work. You can do this with an app such as Cinematic, and in less than a minute you will have a finished video ready to upload. The magic of this process is that students are not always sure whose video will be chosen, so they are eager to go online with their parents to find out.

If you work with secondary school students, the benefits to using Twitter are more practical. Posting homework deadlines and exam schedules offer older students a simple way to stay on top of their work, and is particularly useful for those struggling with the general chaos of adolescence.

## CLASSROOM TWEETS TO THE WIDER COMMUNITY

One aspect of Twitter that goes largely untapped in education is classroom engagement. Twitter enables you to engage with any person, organisation or community in the world that has an account and this can add depth to learning. At primary level, you could supplement geography topics by tweeting questions to the World Wildlife Fund or Greenpeace, or even send them examples of students' classwork. At secondary level, you could support history by following @WorldWarII for real time tweets of events from the same day between 1943-46.

The important point to take away is that social media changes and broadens the definition of what communities are. As part of my business studies A Level coursework in 2004 I had to write a business plan for my own imaginary business. I used the local video store as the blueprint because this was as far as my community reached. Communities today now stretch beyond geographical limitations. Students can interact with Apple in California, or speak with Nike in Oregon. They can even speak to astronauts on the International Space Station! With the ability to interact with anyone, anywhere, the possibilities for deepening learning are almost limitless.

## CREATING A SOCIAL MEDIA POSTING POLICY

Social media is a scary proposition for many schools. A Lot of leadership teams avoid it altogether because of their concerns over e-safety. In reality, there are relatively few risk when **posting** to social media. The risk occur when **browsing** social media, which is **not** how you would be using Twitter. What minimal risks you face can easily be mitigated by creating a posting policy. This is a set of rules for any school member posting content. It should answer the following questions:

- Are we allowed to post pictures including children's faces?
- Are we allowed to name children in posts?
- What type of content are we allowed to post?
- What type of comments can we make on posts?

The first step to getting Twitter up and running is to gauge how many teachers are happy to be involved. There is no limit on this because the more included the better. Only having one teacher involved means your school's Twitter feed will only engage with the parents from that one class. The goal is to engage the whole parental community, so you will need multiple teachers involved.

The best school Twitter feeds post regular updates. Setting up a Twitter profile and posting once per week is little use because parents simply lose interest. I see this often in schools using

Twitter. My advice is to fully commit to the social media project or skip it altogether. Ideally, you want at least one post going out each day. The more staff you have using Twitter, the easier this becomes. The biggest concern I hear from teachers is that they will *'mess something up.'* Alleviate any worries by creating a posting policy and develop an easy-to-follow posting workflow. There are two very useful free apps that you should build your posting workflow around:

**Buffer**

Buffer is a scheduling app that enables you to schedule when your tweets to go out. Rather than posting directly via Twitter, you use the Buffer app to compose your post and leave it to send at the scheduled time. The benefit of this is that you can review all tweets before they are live, while getting the maximum engagement by posting when parents are most likely to be online. There is little point tweeting at 9.15am when few parents are free to read the post!

Using a scheduled posting workflow should allay teachers' worries about posting something that may come back to haunt them and might just convince a senior leader of the benefits of social media. If you set up the posting workflow I have outlined here, you can demonstrate that there is a managed process in place and that all content can be reviewed before anything goes live.

## Skitch

Skitch is a photo-editing app that is part of Evernote, an excellent online note-taking programme. A simple tap of the screen allows you to pixelate part of any image, which means you can anonymise students if you do not have their parents' permission to photograph them.

## KEY TAKEAWAYS

- Transforming a school with iPads is not just about getting more out of every lesson. It is about getting more out of the whole day, and when the iPad goes home it means learning does too. Inform parents of your project's goals and explain the benefits in depth at the earliest possible opportunity. Make them allies for learning at home.

- Use social media to communicate with parents. Aim to provoke their interest in their child's learning with fun and informative tweets.

- If students are taking their iPads home, make it compulsory for parents to attend an evening at the school. This is a perfect way of reaching those parents who are not attending parent evenings or responding to school communications.

# THE TABLET REVOLUTION

# Chapter 13
# LEARNING FRAMEWORKS

To improve learning opportunities for students, schools need to embrace pedagogical evolution. In other words, growth and change in **how** you teach, as well as **what** you teach. This culture shift can be one of the most challenging aspects of creating an iPad project, and it is worth taking a step back and thinking about how you will manage this as a team.

## SHIFTING CULTURES

To enable your school's teaching methods to evolve, it is vital to understand the individual needs of your staff. Pay attention to their priorities, and take time to consider the ways iPads can benefit and help them to achieve these. For example, Surbiton High, which runs a full scale 1:1 project, does this very well, allocating development time to staff independently from group sessions. This brings a personalised learning touch to staff development.

This chapter explores three learning frameworks that will help you to clarify your staff's training and development needs. Each framework should help you to understand what the school has already achieved and what it needs to do next in terms of the learning pedagogy. The first is *The Stages of Learning Cycle,* a model for everyone to use. Teachers can use it to evaluate their own learning and project leaders can use it to evaluate how staff are progressing. The second is TPACK, a model for project leaders to assess the progress of the iPad project. The third is SAMR, a model that teachers can use to self assess their use of technology in the classroom.

Before I introduce these frameworks, however, I want to explain how to carry out a skills audit, because you will need to know your staff's basic skill level before you can evaluate their training needs.

## SKILLS AUDIT

A good place to start is to assess all teachers' skill and ability level using mobile technology. Just because teachers use tablets in their personal life, this does not mean they will know how to use the same technology in the classroom. I have worked with schools that have made this assumption, and were left with a workforce that felt under-supported and under-equipped to take part in its technological revolution as a result.

Your skills audit should assess two critical aspects of learning: **confidence** and **competence**. Assessing confidence is straightforward, and you can do this by asking respondents to rate their confidence with technology on a scale of 1 to 10. A Google Forms quiz would be sufficient here. It may come as a surprise to see how many of your staff lack confidence when using technology. Many teachers I speak to feel apprehensive about introducing iPads into lessons, and find the idea of using new teaching methods intimidating.

To measure competency, ask teachers how able they are to use the iPad for tasks you need them to be proficient in. Again, use a sliding scale. Here are some examples:

*i) How competent are you at using the Explain Everything app?*
Totally Unable         Somewhat Able         Very Able
1     2     3     4     5     6     7     8     9     10


*ii) How competent are you at using the camera app to take pictures and record video?*

| Totally Unable | | | | Somewhat Able | | | | Very Able | |
|---|---|---|---|---|---|---|---|---|---|
| 1 | 2 | 3 | 4 | 5 | 6 | 7 | 8 | 9 | 10 |

*iii) How competent are you to saving work and moving files to and from the iPad?*

| Totally Unable | | | | Somewhat Able | | | | Very Able | |
|---|---|---|---|---|---|---|---|---|---|
| 1 | 2 | 3 | 4 | 5 | 6 | 7 | 8 | 9 | 10 |

Keep the statements generic, as anything too specific will skew the results of your audit.

Now that your skills audit is complete, you should have an understanding of the overall skill level in your school. This will identify where the most work is needed. For a better understanding of your staff's learning needs, you can use the three models that follow, starting with the *Stages of Learning Cycle*.

## 1. THE STAGES OF LEARNING CYCLE

For any skills-based training, the Stages of Learning cycle is an invaluable tool. It offers a means to assess staff competence in a particular area. Before I explain each stage of the cycle, it is important to clarify that I want you to use the Stages of Learning cycle to gauge **pedagogical competence**, not **technical skill**. Pedagogical competence has two components: the knowledge of how to teach and improve learning using an iPad and the skill to do so. Here is an example of a teacher who has both:

### Miss Brown: pedagogically competent

*Miss Brown has pedagogical knowledge because she understands that to increase student engagement within history, she can use Showbie to mark work faster and give deeper feedback. She knows that this should increase engagement because she is able to improve and increase the interactions she has with students through the assessment process, and that the quicker she can return work the better she can challenge and develop students' understanding.*

In this example, Miss Brown also requires the technical skills to use Showbie in order to engage better with students. However, Miss Brown understands that it is not Showbie that is extending learning opportunities for her students, but her input in the form of feedback and guidance via Showbie that makes the difference. It is important to understand the difference between **pedagogical skill** and **technical skill**, and best to keep these two concepts separate.

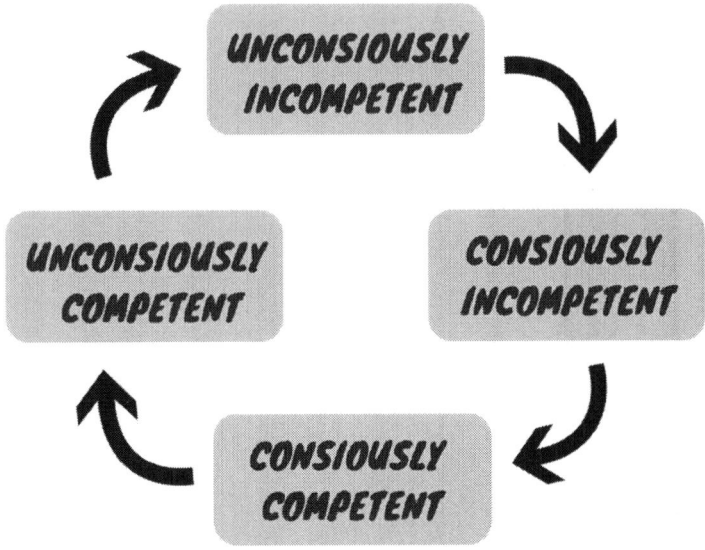

The Stages of Learning Cycle

At the beginning of your iPad project, teachers are most likely to be *unconsciously incompetent* (**stage 1**). In simple terms, they do not know what it is they are trying to learn. Teachers can only unlock the potential of the iPad if they understand what the potential is. They can progress from stage 1 to stage 2 (see below) by reading articles, blogs or publications on effective use of mobile devices, or by seeing other teachers using technology effectively.

In **stage 2,** staff are *consciously incompetent:* they know what they are trying to learn. They understand how the iPad can improve learning, but do not possess the pedagogical skill to begin doing so. Moving beyond this stage is difficult without a staff development programme.

In **stage 3** staff become *consciously competent:* they know that they have reached a level of mastery with the iPad. Typically this is achieved through support, guidance and sustained development. It is not necessary to progress beyond being *consciously competent,* and in many ways this is the prime stage for long term success.

In **stage 4,** staff are *unconsciously competent.* You might call someone at this stage a 'natural', a person who is very good at something, but cannot necessarily explain how they do it. I would be wary of choosing a Stage 4 'natural' to lead your school training. A teacher may be the most gifted at using an iPads with students, but if they can't explain their methods, they may be unable to develop other staff, rendering their leadership counterproductive. Take a leaf out of the sports world and prioritise coaching ability over performance ability. Many of the greatest football managers were average players at best, while many of the greatest players make average managers. This is often attributed to the fact that great individuals were great from a young age *(unconsciously competent)* and find it difficult to appreciate and develop those who are not.

| Stage | Do they **know** how to use the technology to improve learning? | Do they possess the **pedagogical** skill to improve learning? |
|---|---|---|
| Unconsciously incompetent | No | No |
| Consciously incompetent | Yes | No |
| Consciously competent | Yes | Yes |
| Unconsciously competent | Yes | Yes |

## Sustained development

The beauty of the Stages of Learning cycle is that its structure serves to remind us that learning is a process with many phases to it. Technology-focused CPD, in contrast to what the learning cycle teaches, is typically delivered in one-off training sessions, so there is little opportunity for teachers to develop their knowledge and skills. In May 2012, the Teacher Development Trust found that "in order to effectively address pupils' learning needs, teachers need to keep practising, adapting and refining their new ideas regularly, for at least two terms and ideally longer." With anything less than 30 hours practice, reflection and refinement, improvements risked being lost. On that evidence, three hours sat in an INSET training session equates to just 10% of the time required to bring about improvement.

The Stages of Learning Cycle has further relevance as it focuses development on pedagogical competence over technological skill. The truth is, it is not about what apps you use in the classroom, but how you use the iPad effectively; in other words, how to differentiate, engage and improve student learning with a mobile device. Unfortunately, a lot of iPad training available to schools focuses solely on apps. It is often seen as easier to send a teacher on a course in which they will cover twenty iPad apps than it is to send them on a course to develop their pedagogical knowledge. Whilst it may be easier, it is an approach that reaps little reward. Avoid falling into the trap of becoming an app-focused school.

The key to long-term success is to develop pedagogical skill throughout your school. Not every member of staff has to become an expert at planning iPad lessons, but if the majority has even a basic knowledge of the pedagogy to deliver key learning outcomes, the school will achieve far more than it would by sending teachers on all the app training in the world.

## 2. THE TPACK MODEL

The TPACK model was created in 1986 by Lee Shulman. It is used by school districts in America to develop the impact of technology on learning. Most schools I have worked with are unfamiliar with the model, so do not be put off if it is new to you. In the US, school districts decide what technology to buy and deploy it to all of their schools. The costs for districts reach the hundreds of millions, so they are very keen on frameworks that can develop the technology's impact once it is in classrooms.

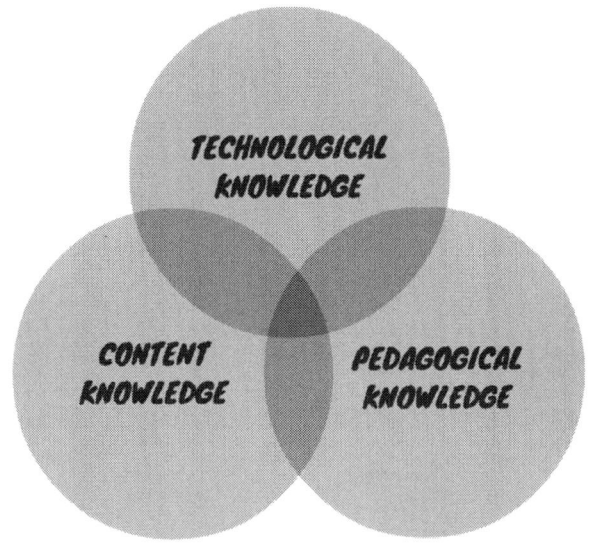

The TPACK Model

TPACK stands for **T**echnological knowledge, **P**edagogical knowledge **A**nd **C**ontent **K**nowledge. I have used the simplified version of the TPACK model above, because only these three areas should apply to you. The aim is for your project to sit in the centre of the Venn diagram, where technological, pedagogical and content knowledge meet. If you can achieve this, I am confident that the outcome will be positive.

**Technological Knowledge**

The first element is to have the right equipment to do the job. This means you need to choose the right device for your school, install a wireless system in top-notch condition, and find solutions to save and share work. Much of this information is covered in the Infrastructure chapter.

**Pedagogical Knowledge**

Alongside infrastructure and devices, you also need to understand how to embed the iPad into your curriculum. Without this knowledge, none of the school's expensive technology will make any difference. The biggest challenge for most schools is that staff are just not aware of what they should be using the iPad for; they are *unconsciously incompetent*, if you will. It is vital to think about how you will upskill teachers to develop the knowledge and understanding they require. Remember that the iPad by itself provides no impact on learning.

**Content Knowledge**

The final piece of the puzzle is having content to take advantage of the new technology. In your project's initial stages, content might be app-focused, and a direct replacement for paper or laptop-based activities. This must only be a short-term measure; you need to make time to generate content that takes advantages of the iPad's potential. I cover this in depth in the Learning Evolved chapter.

Now that you have a better understanding of each component in the TPACK framework, you should have recognised that this is not for the everyday teacher. This is the remit of the project leader, whose goal is to be the strategic thinker, planning the steps ahead for the institution.

## 3. THE SAMR MODEL

SAMR is an acronym for **S**ubstitution, **A**ugmentation, **M**odification and **R**edefinition. The model acts as an evaluation scale from which teachers can assess their own use of technology in their teaching.

## The SAMR Model

**TRANSFORMATION**

**REDEFINITION**
Tech allows for the creation of new tasks, previously inconceivable

**MODIFICATION**
Tech allows for significant task design

**ENHANCEMENT**

**AUGMENTATION**
Tech acts as a direct tool substitution, with functional change

**SUBSTITUTION**
Tech acts as a direct tool substitution, with no functional change

To get us started, I will use an example to demonstrate how to apply the model.

**Example Task**: Students are reading Romeo & Juliet for GCSE English

| Stage | Description | Action |
|---|---|---|
| Substitution | Tech acts as a direct tool substitute with no functional change | Students read Romeo & Juliet on the iPad instead of a book |
| Augmentation | Tech acts as a direct tool substitute with functional improvement | Using the iBooks app, students can use the inbuilt dictionary, search Wikipedia and make detailed notes all within the app |
| Modification | Tech allows for significant task redesign | Students create their own digital books, perhaps exploring the themes of Romeo & Juliet by writing a modern equivalent |
| Redefinition | Tech allows for the creation of new tasks, previously inconceivable | Using the iPad students can add interactive media content into their digital book such as videos, audio or widgets |

The aim of the SAMR model is to raise teachers' self-awareness of how they use technology in their classroom. I am a firm believer that technology should be used to provide functional improvements to learning. If a school replaces laptops with iPads, but then only uses those iPads for web browsing, no functional improvement has taken place. The technology has merely been *substituted*, because the task could have been completed with the old laptops. If students in another school use their iPads to act out and film scenes from Romeo and Juliet, the iPad is now delivering functional improvements because the learning activity has been *redefined*.

One word of warning when using the SAMR model; it is not a ladder and teachers should not feel pressured to reach the *Redefinition* stage. While many activities undertaken at this stage are more engaging and immersive for students, they also require a lot more time. Teachers and schools are time-poor, and it is unrealistic to attempt to redefine *all* of your teaching just because you now have an iPad. It is about finding the right balance. A healthy approach is to target subject knowledge that students have difficulty understanding. Many primary schools have difficulty teaching students grammar rules because it is such a dry subject. This represents a perfect opportunity to *redefine* learning using the iPad. This could be done by grouping students together and tasking them with making a grammar infomercial in which they have to teach others how to use specific grammar elements. By creating an experience for students, it increases their involvement in learning which is more likely to boost later recall.

Now that we understand that not everything should be redefined in the classroom, I will also point out that not all substitution tasks are a waste of the technology. SAMR can attract purists who state that you should always be moving through the model towards redefinition, but this is not the case. Here are some useful examples:

**Benefits of substitution tasks**

**Example Task**: Students are reading Romeo & Juliet for GCSE English

- **Improved access:** Having a digital copy of Romeo & Juliet increases student access because the book is accessible at any time they have the iPad. A physical book will often stay in class, and even when the student owns a copy, it is only likely to be with them on the days they are required to bring it.
- **Increased lesson time:** If it takes 5 minutes to hand out and collect all books within an English lesson, over the course of a school year that amounts to around 8 hours (depending on your school's own timetable) in total. Reading from a digital copy, as long as the iPads do not need to be handed out, will save this time each lesson, thus maximising available learning.
- **Free updates and no replacement costs:** This applies more to textbooks than literature, but it is still relevant. When you buy a digital textbook, you will receive lifetime updates, so no more decade old textbooks for your students! Neither can

digital copies be damaged, defaced or worn down, removing the need to buy replacements as the years go by.

- **Reduced cost per book:** With no physical manufacturing process you will not be surprised to hear that the majority of digital textbooks are cheaper than their physical counterparts.
- **Project Gutenberg:** Any literature that is over 75 years old, and is registered under Project Gutenberg is available free of charge as a digital copy as it is out of copyright. This includes Shakespeare's works and many other key English curriculum texts.

In many projects, technology is only deployed to deliver educational benefits, and this can lead institutions to miss the cost saving benefits that even simple substitution tasks can provide. The key is to look at the whole picture, and unearth the benefits that might have otherwise been missed.

## KEY TAKEAWAYS

- Frameworks are your friends. Working through them can greatly aid the development of teachers and staff on your iPad project.

- TPACK should be the responsibility of the strategic thinkers and project leaders. Do not underestimate the technological knowledge you require, and include your infrastructure within that section. Many schools forget to address their wireless network capabilities and find that it does not adequately support iPads once the project starts. That can lead to disaster. Do not fall into the trap!

- The more teachers that are aware of the SAMR model, the better iPad use is likely to be within classrooms. SAMR provides an easy to use framework from which teachers can self assess. However, be aware that it is not a race to the redefinition stage. iPad projects should be about improving and building upon what you are already doing, not tearing up the rule book and starting again.

# Chapter 14

# STAFF DEVELOPMENT

It is worth taking to heart the following mantra for your iPad project:

> *Technology alone delivers no impact or improvement on learning. It is teachers who have the power to transform education.*

Before you start to grapple with the iPad, remember that it is merely another learning tool, albeit one with enormous potential.

There is no school that I know of that is better than its teachers. It does not matter how strong your vision is or how developed your infrastructure may be, without strong and sustained staff development, it will all be for nothing. I encourage you to think of professional development as an investment rather than a cost, because it is the only way that your endeavours to improve learning will have lasting impact.

The last equipment to see such widespread adoption in education was interactive whiteboards, and over a decade after their rapid adoption, they have proved to be nothing more than a white elephant. Interactive whiteboards could have improved learning, but they rarely did because adequate money was not spent on training teachers in how to use them. From my experience, the majority of teachers use them solely to project their computer to the front of the class. For the most part, the rest of their potential remains untapped.

The same will happen to your project if you ignore the importance of staff development. Invest in quality training to ensure the iPad is not just another white elephant.

Staff development is a wide topic. I will focus on:

1. Why you should prioritise 25% of your project's budget into staff development
2. Why you should prioritise the development of pedagogy and assessment over curriculum

## PRIORITISING STAFF DEVELOPMENT

I have noticed a spending ratio that features time and again in all the good iPad projects when it comes to training: the successful schools allocate at least 25% of the project's total cost towards a training resource.

As highlighted by the Teacher Development Trust, it takes a teacher at least 30 hours of practice, reflection and enquiry before training impacts on the needs and requirements of a student. A single INSET or twilight training session is nowhere near enough, and any successful training programme for your school should focus on the long term development. Let us have a look at the following scenario:

You have a budget of £10,000 for an iPad Mini project. Your spending options are as follows:

| Option | iPad | Cases | Training |
| --- | --- | --- | --- |
| A | 50 iPad Minis | 0 Cases | 0 Days Training |
| B | 46 iPad Minis | 46 Cases | 0 Days Training |
| C | 35 iPad Minis | 35 Cases | 4 Days Training |

I would always opt for option C, because this will set you up for the journey ahead. However, in my experience, almost all schools will opt for option A or B. When it comes to technology, there is a big preoccupation with amassing resources at the expense of developing teachers. It is painful to recall the number of times I have witnessed this kind of decision making in schools, where staff were impervious to my attempts to encourage investment towards training. It was clear from the outset which of these projects would fail and which would prosper.

The preoccupation with amassing technology over developing staff needs to end if schools are going to make effective use of iPads. The 2015 report *"Students, Computers and Learning: Making The Connection"* found that countries which have invested heavily into information and communication technologies (ICT) over a sustained period in education have seen no noticeable improvement in their performances in PISA results for reading, mathematics or science. This is because education is caught in a technology 'arms race' that is well into its second decade. It started with interactive whiteboards, then moved quickly to laptops, and now has moved on yet again to tablets, with the iPad leading the pack. But, hold on a minute; is there any point to all of this? What have interactive whiteboards and laptops actually done to improve **your** teaching practice? Whenever I ask teachers this question, I am met with blank stares or vague replies about 'student engagement'. The teachers are not to blame for this. As I stated earlier, technology has failed to have an impact because teachers were never sufficiently trained. That rests with the school leadership.

## 25% on staff development! Why so much?

Investing 25% of your year one budget may sound like a big chunk, but it is actually little over the course of the project. Schools tend to think in annual spending cycles, and often do not calculate the lifetime costs associated with running a technology project. Mobile technology is here to stay, and the significant costs become more apparent when you look at the ten-year scenario.

If a school starts with a budget of £200,000, I suggest 25% of that, £50,000, is spent on staff development in year one. On face value, most schools would baulk at spending this much into development alone. However, if we take the cost of the project over a ten-year period into account, things begin to look very different.

**Scenario**: A secondary school with 600 students and 70 teachers wants to become a full 1:1 school. The starting budget is £200,000. Below is a rough spending guide based on the typical prices of each element at the time of writing.

# THE TABLET REVOLUTION

| Spend | Year 1 Cost | Total over 10 years |
|---|---|---|
| 600 student iPad Minis with accessories. Replaced in the fourth and eighth year | £126,000 | £378,000 |
| 70 staff 9.7" iPads with accessories. Replaced in the fourth and eighth year | £20,000 | £60,000 |
| 4 iPad CPD sessions each year | £2600 | £26,000 |
| Wireless Network upgrade | | £15,000 - 50,000 |
| Breakages and replacements | £3420 - 5700 | £34,200 - 57,000 |
| MDM system | £4200 | £42,000 |
| IT technician | £15,000 - 25,000 | £150,000 - 250,000 |
| Apps, software and misc purchases | £1000 - 3000 | £10,000 - 30,000 |
| Grand Total | £158,720 - 173,000 | £715,200 - 893,000 |

Assuming the school is putting on external iPad training sessions for staff each year as many do, this will add up to about £26,000 over ten years. My suggestion is that £50,000 is spent in year one, in order to develop the leadership capabilities of an iPad strategic team and make the school self-sufficient. No external training providers would be required under this scenario, therefore saving the school £26,000 over the ten year period. This £26,000 saving can be offset against the initial £50,000 spent in year one. This means the **true** cost is only £24,000 to become self-sufficient and give your project the best chance of succeeding.

If you still think spending £24,000 in this scenario is too much, look at it another way. £24,000 equates to less than 3% of the expected ten-year spend.

**The exception to the rule**

It is possible that your school does not require this level of investment. Occasionally, a project leader comes along with the expertise and vision necessary to develop an internal training programme. Abdul Chohan and Greg Hughes did exactly this at ESSA Academy and The de Ferrers Academy respectively, and their leadership qualities made their 1:1 schemes resounding successes. Note that these two are the exception rather than the rule, and unless you have the technological visionaries within your school with the time and resources to develop the project, I would budget 25% instead.

## WHAT KIND OF TRAINING?

There are three areas you can focus training and development into. These are:

| CURRICULUM | PEDAGOGY | ASSESSMENT |
|---|---|---|
| What students are taught | How students are taught | The evaluation of student's learning |

In most iPad projects I have come across, training is focused almost exclusively towards curriculum. In other words, teachers are shown different versions of curriculum content they already deliver, such as digitised worksheets instead of paper ones.

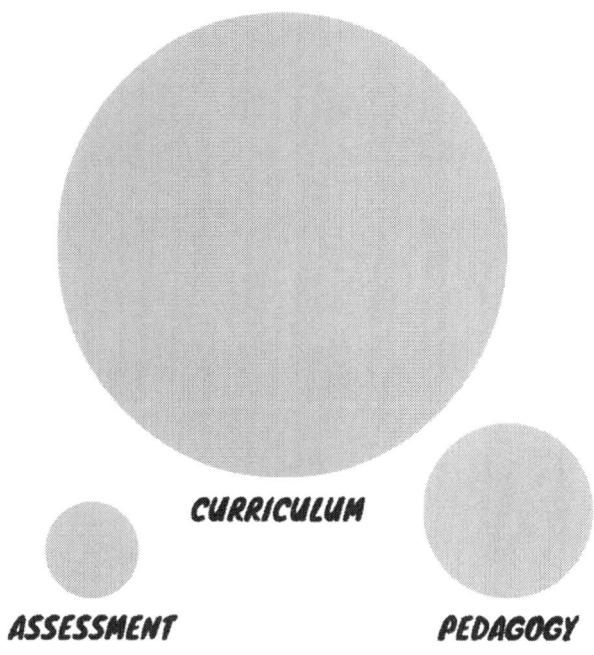

I urge you to buck the trend and avoid this weighting, because it is a very ineffective way to spend your time and money. When you prioritise curriculum training, your teachers spend their time learning skills, content and activities that may only be relevant to handful of their lessons. Much of this type of training is app specific, and while it does provide teachers with valuable skills, it is not always applicable to every lesson. When you have a finite training budget you want to get the most from your money.

I recommend you prioritise your staff development like this:

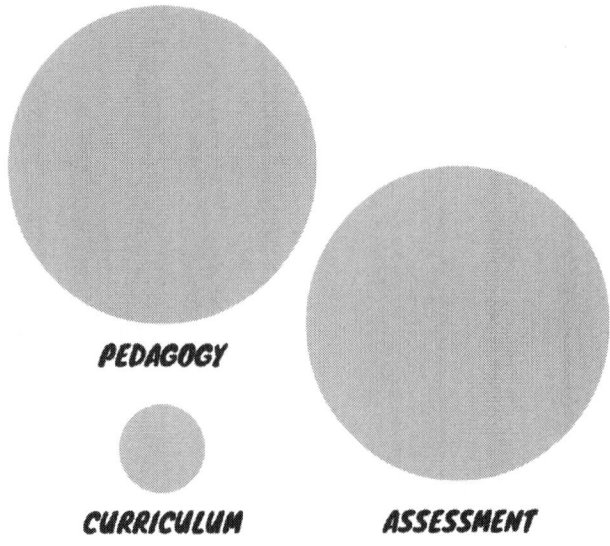

You want to prioritise pedagogy and assessment because these affect every lesson. Pedagogy has long been recognised as the biggest factor on student performance. Any good educator understands that the way a student is taught is more important than the resources at hand. As for assessment, it is one of the most time-consuming elements of teaching. If assessment can be sped up (and it can significantly), this creates more time for teachers to do what they are best at - developing rich and engaging lessons for their students!

Focus on developing pedagogy and assessment, and you will find that the curriculum will look after itself. Let's look at why in more detail.

## CURRICULUM VS. PEDAGOGY

Should you focus on learning the best apps for each individual subject? Most definitely not! Allocating a portion of training time to basic device training is important to ensure staff are comfortable and confident with the technology. Using the rest to learn about apps is a sure-fire way to minimise any return from your investment. The only apps you should be focused on are those that allow you to create content or deepen engagement, because these offer a fundamental advancement to classroom tasks and can be used across all subjects. Any other type of app is simply a replacement for an existing process, nothing more than a *'digital worksheet'*.

The better focus is to prioritise as much of your training allowance into developing pedagogical knowledge and skills with teachers. Remember that strategic iPad team I was going on about earlier in the book? This is where they become invaluable to the long term development of your project. If you prioritise training that group first, within a short amount of time you will have a highly-trained core of teachers able to support and train the rest of the staff. Taking this route will allow you to develop a sustained training programme as you reduce your reliance on external expertise. Let us take a look at the options logically one-by-one.

**Scenario**: To train 30 teaching staff, 5 of which are on the iPad Strategic Team.

| Option | Training mix | Advantages | Disadvantages |
| --- | --- | --- | --- |
| A - Whole School Approach | 3x inset days + 2x twilights | Staff develop together at the same time.<br><br>All staff feel like they are being invested in and supported.<br><br>Instant takeaway ideas and uses for iPad in the classroom. | Ability range of whole school training can reduce impact. Sessions can be too fast for some but too slow for others.<br><br>One-size-fits-all training reduces relevance for individual subjects.<br><br>Learning stops once training is complete. |

| | | | |
|---|---|---|---|
| B - Mixed School Approach | 2x inset days + 2x iPad team days | Advantages of a whole school approach while also beginning to develop a iPad Team.<br><br>Beginnings of creating a culture of innovation by upskilling iPad Team | Similar disadvantages to a whole school approach.<br><br>iPad Team will need to become experts, and that requires a significant investment of time and support. |
| C - Top Down Approach | 4x iPad team days | Significant investment in iPad Team will go a long way to developing expertise.<br><br>A successful iPad Team will create their own innovation, and will be able to lead future training sessions | Staff who are not on the iPad Team may feel unsupported (in the short term).<br><br>Requires a longer term approach. |

Most schools prioritise option A, the whole school approach. I ran a training session with a collection of primary schools one time that had almost one hundred teachers in. I got through about 10% of what I usually do because the ability range was so wide that there were endless questions and stoppages. The best option is to select C. It enables your school to become self-sufficient, with members of the iPad Team leading future training sessions. This removes any budgetary limitations that may exist for staff development, while simultaneously increasing your training provision.

There is no shortcut to developing deeper pedagogical understanding for teachers. If you teach staff how to use one app, you can support them through one lesson; give them pedagogical understanding and you can support them to transform their classrooms throughout the year.

## ASSESSMENT

I mentioned earlier that it is possible to significantly speed up the assessment process in schools. This is done by digitising assessment. There are two methods to achieving this.

|  | Paperless Method | 'Hacked' Method |
|---|---|---|
| Devices per class | Teacher + all students | Teacher only |
| Workflow | Students complete work digitally on their iPad before submitted it to a digital assessment platform such as Showbie. The teacher marks the work and the student receives it back online. | Students complete work on paper, and the teacher photographs the work and uploads it to a digital assessment platform. This 'digitises' the work. The teacher marks the work and the student receives it back online. |
| Pros | All students have access to digital assessment platform through their iPad. | Incredible low cost. Students utilise their own device (phone, tablet, computer) or the school's IT provision to receive work back. |
| Cons | Expensive to equip all students with iPads. All students must have an iPad for workflow to work. | If students cannot get online at home another provision must be put in place for them. |

Refer to the Broadgreen case study on page 242 for more details.

## KEY TAKEAWAYS

- Prioritise pedagogy and assessment development over curriculum. Transforming student learning is more about **how** they learn rather than **what** they learn.

- Rethink your initial training allocation because it is almost never enough. The most successful projects invest about 25% of their project budget into staff development. If you want to achieve similar levels of success, then be prepared to do the same.

- An iPad Strategic Team is an invaluable asset to any project, and you should make it your top priority to develop one. Focus your training on developing a core team of staff to become skilled and pedagogy-savvy. This will enable your school to become self sufficient and lead its own professional development.

# Chapter 15

# FINDING THE RIGHT TRAINER

## APPLE PROFESSIONAL DEVELOPMENT

In the Selecting the Right Supplier chapter I recommended buying your iPads from a Apple Solution Expert or ASE, a company certified to sell Apple products. If you choose to do so, you are entitled to a half-day training session called Apple Professional Development (APD) for every 25 iPads you purchase. APD training is always delivered by an Apple-certified AET (Apple Educational Trainer) and can be a great bonus for your school, especially if you are on a tight budget. Bear in mind, however that Apple Professional Development training should only be **part** of your training plan and not your **whole** training plan. It is important to make the best use of your time with an AET by taking the initiative and working with one who has the best level of expertise for your school's needs.

The first thing to understand about Apple Professional Development training is that it is strictly regulated by Apple. Up until recently, trainers had to deliver a set course from Apple's Professional Development catalogue. In 2015, Apple introduced a *'mentoring'* course that allows selected Apple Educational Trainers to deliver training more suited to the school's requirements. In total there are less than 70 AETs in the country, and not all of them are certified to deliver the mentoring course. This means you do not actually have a great deal of choice.

The majority of Apple Solution Experts have their own in-house AETs and currently, unless you specify otherwise, the in-house AET will deliver your training. You are entitled to choose your own trainer, and I would strongly encourage more schools to exercise this right, because their skill set and professional experience varies widely. Do you want a trainer who has taught in secondary or primary school? Do you want one with a history of school leadership? These are the types of questions you will need to ask yourself.

To understand which trainer is best for you, it is important to know a little bit more about the AET appointment process. The experience of an AET will depend on when they were appointed. Apple recruited AETs in three waves:.

**First wave:** Apple recruited professionals who worked in and around education. Some were teachers, but many were from City Learning Centres or ICT support roles.

**Second Wave:** Apple required applicants to have five years of teaching experience to apply in order to ensure greater pedagogical knowledge amongst the trainers.

**Third wave:** Applicants need five years of teaching experience and leadership-level experience at a school. This was designed to ensure trainers could advise on leadership and strategy, as well as pedagogy.

## GOING OUTSIDE THE APPLE NETWORK

**Curriculum and Pedagogical Development**

Curriculum and pedagogy are both are hot topics in education, and I am yet to meet a trainer who does not offer to impart training and expertise on both. However, developing these two areas requires a long-term strategy and intricate understanding of school development (see Learning Frameworks and Staff Development chapters). When hiring a trainer, **always** look at their track record and ask for references that evidence their work has had measurable impact. It might surprise you how few trainers are able to provide this.

Yet, I frequently visit schools who receive training from individuals who have never taught. How can someone help you develop pedagogy and curriculum if they have never done the job first hand? It is a sure-fire way to minimise any impact from your budget, so never be afraid to question a trainer's background, and do not be afraid to say 'no'. You have a limited budget, so use it wisely.

One of the barriers to finding good trainers is the lack of easily accessible networks of companies or individuals nationwide that do this type of work. Currently, the best way to find a trainer in this area is good old fashioned networking. Ask local schools who are using iPads to recommend a trainer, or take to Twitter and pose the question to fellow educators. A useful tip is to use #ADEchat hashtag as this is a global network of Apple Distinguished Educators and they are likely to have a collective deep knowledge in this area.

## KEY TAKEAWAY

- Apple Professional Development training should make up part of your training plan, not all of it. Look at it as a bonus.

- Always question a trainer's expertise and track record. If I tell you a football team played 38 games last season, then you have no idea how good they. It is an irrelevant stat. They could have lost every game! This is no different from trainers who have worked with hundreds of schools and trained thousands of teachers. What is the impact? After all, you are hiring them to deliver impact for you, not to become the 101st school they have trained.

- Do not be afraid to ask for someone other than the ASE appointed trainer when you buy your iPads. You want the best for your school, and their appointed trainer just may not have the experience you need.

# THE TABLET REVOLUTION

## Chapter 16
# BEHAVIOUR IN THE CLASSROOM

One area that has the potential to put staff on edge during any iPad project is how to cope with behaviour management once devices are unleashed in the classrooms. The journey towards mobile learning is a big cultural shift and with Google, Wikipedia and YouTube only a few clicks away, a teacher is no longer the sole fountain of knowledge in the room. This creates anxiety amongst some teachers that students may become disruptive and difficult to manage. If the thought of this makes you break out into a cold sweat, the following advice will be worth keeping in mind.

## MANAGING BEHAVIOUR AS A TEAM

One of the best pieces of advice I have heard on the issue of iPads and behaviour came from my colleague James Hannam:

*"Manage behaviour, not devices."*

There are two key times during your project when you will need to prepare for possible behaviour issues. The first is before the iPads enter the classroom; the second is once the iPads are in the students' hands. The former should be the responsibility of the Project Leader; the latter responsibility is that of classroom teachers.

## BEFORE THE IPADS REACH THE CLASSROOM

The more carefully the project leader prepares their school for the switch over to iPads, the better teachers will be able to manage possible changes in students' behaviour. As long as you have considered the possible negative impact on behaviour and protected against it, there is no reason why managing behaviour should be any more taxing than usual.

As Project Leader, two strategies will help you with this:

**a. Draw clear lines of responsibility**

From the outset of the project, you need to draw clear lines of responsibility for the relevant stakeholders in school. The most successful projects draw responsibility up as follows:

- The technical team is there to ensure apps, content and workflows are in place and working when the devices are called into action.
- The teaching team is there to teach and manage behaviour within lessons.
- The students are there to learn. They get to use the device on the basis that they use it responsibly.

Do not hand over the responsibility of managing behaviour to your technical team. Some schools try to manage iPads like PCs and put them in 'lockdown' mode. This invariably fails because the iPad is not designed to be managed this way; it is a single sign-on system and cannot be managed and tracked via an administrative account as PCs can. This approach also dulls the impact on learning. The more you *'lock'* the device down, the more you reduce its potential in the classroom. If you are not careful, you can end up with nothing but glorified e-readers!

### b. Create an Acceptable User Policy

An Acceptable User Policy (AUP) outlines the responsibilities of students when using their iPads, and gives clear guidelines for managing behaviour and issuing sanctions when required. It can be created as part of your school's e-safety policy. Make it mandatory for all students to sign the policy before using an iPad and, if students are taking iPads home, extend this requirement to their parents. It is worth taking the time to speak to parents about these responsibilities even if you do not intend to let students take their device home. The more support for the policy you have from parents, the less likely it is that behaviour problems will occur.

An AUP is in essence a contract that requires students to use iPads appropriately. One of the best AUPs I have seen was created by Gavin Holden, project leader at Abbot Beyne School. It includes an *'iPassport'* that requires students to work through and demonstrate key competencies with their iPad before they are allowed to take it home. This creates a clear incentive for students to behave with their device in lessons, and because it takes a number of weeks to complete all *'iPassport'* competencies, it ensures students form good classroom habits from the outset.

## IN THE CLASSROOM

Once the iPads are live in the classroom, there are some simple techniques that teachers can use to keep them from becoming a distraction. Apple's introduction of their Classroom app, part of the iOS 9.3 update, gives teachers the ability to lock students into particular apps and remote view their screens. This goes a long way to improving behaviour management in lessons but it should not be used as a *'managing from the front'* policy as has been the case with previous school technology. The strategies that worked best before iPads entered the classroom are still most effective. Here are a few examples:

**1. Untether yourself from the desk**

To manage the classroom effectively, free yourself from your desk! Moving around the room makes it easier to spot students who are struggling or misbehaving. Make sure you put a solution in place that will allow you to wirelessly mirror (AirPlay) your iPad to the display in the classroom. I covered the most popular options in the Infrastructure chapter.

**2. The countdown method**

*"3, 2, 1 show me your iPad screen."* Have all students hold up their device, screen forward (another reason it is important to have a robust case on all devices) to check they are on task. This is a

simple yet great classroom management tactic because there is nowhere to hide. If a certain student is slow in presenting their screen or furiously clicking or swiping, then you can be pretty sure they are not doing what you have asked of them. From there you can have the relevant conversation.

**3. The paper alternative method**

It is only natural that students will get excited when using iPads for the first time in lessons, and it is important to temper that excitement by setting the right tone. Students like to test boundaries, and another deterrent to misbehaviour is by having a paper alternative of the task you are undertaking with the iPad. If a student ignores your warnings, they lose the use of an iPad for a set time (ranging from 5 minutes to the whole lesson) and you issue them with a paper-based copy of the task. They are unlikely to want to be the only one without an iPad in the lesson, and even if they do not heed your warnings in the first lesson, they are unlikely to become a repeat offender for fear of missing out.

**4. Guided Access mode**

If your school does not have the Classroom app on your iPads then there is an alternative method to locking students into apps. It is called Guided Access and should only be used as a last resort. '*Blocking out*' the navigation buttons within an app means the student cannot navigate out of the selected page. They will also be locked into the app itself, as the home button is disabled.

In the schools I have worked with, this has proved to be a useful technique for teaching assistants working on an individual basis. Do remember that you need to exit Guided Access before the student or iPad finishes the lesson. It is worth noting that a password should be agreed for the whole school as it is easy to place the iPad back into school circulation locked in Guided Access mode, and this can render the device useless for other teachers.

## KEY TAKEAWAYS

- Behaviour management should always be carried out at the coalface in the classroom. It is not the responsibility of your IT department and, if you make it so, you have already lost the battle.

- Develop an Acceptable User Policy (AUP) so students understand their responsibilities when using the iPad in the classroom. Engage with parents through this process if you have the opportunity.

- Create a behaviour management protocol for the whole school. This will minimise how often students test boundaries in lesson time and empower all teachers to take the right sanctions when enforcing the AUP.

# Chapter 17

# APPS AND WORKFLOW

The majority of iPad training for schools teaches educators how to use apps, and is easily cut and pasted into lessons. Unfortunately, having an arsenal of apps will not transform learning if they do not aid *how* students are learning. This is why it is vital for school leadership to set the tone of the project, and to prioritise the use of apps that allow for deeper learning to take place.

Selected well and used appropriately, apps do have the capability to transform many aspects of learning, from how content is delivered, right through to how students engage with the curriculum. It is all about which apps you choose and how they are used. In the first section of this chapter, I will show you what kinds of apps are out there, which ones to go for and which to avoid. I conclude the chapter by focusing on a framework that will help you to shape how you use apps to improve workflow and efficiency, which I have called CASC (**C**reation, **As**sessment and **C**uration).

## NOT ALL APPS ARE CREATED EQUAL

I like to group apps into three categories: redefining apps, engagement apps and digital worksheet apps. Understanding the difference will help you select which to use in the classroom.

### 1. Redefining apps

At the top of the tree sit apps that redefine the classroom. These are the apps that enable you to undertake new tasks or processes that were previously beyond your reach. Generally any app that allows you to create digital content falls into this category. The iPad films high definition video right out of the box, and combined with apps such as iMovie and DoInk (a greenscreen app) it allows you to develop a wealth of learning activities. Instead of handing in essays or creating posters, you could have students create their own news reports, adverts or movies using real footage cut in with the help of greenscreen.

At primary level, I have seen this used to great effect for developing speaking and listening skills, and persuasive writing. At secondary level, these tools can be used to cement a module or a year's worth of learning into a single project by asking students to look at the body of knowledge and pick what they feel is most relevant for a five minute summary video. Rachel Smith, Modern Foreign Languages and digital lead at Ramsey Grammar School redefined how she taught GCSE French grammar by having students make stop-motion movies to demonstrate their understanding and knowledge. This is then posted to Twitter for parents (and me!) to admire. It is one of the most engaging uses of an iPad I have ever seen, and thirteen years after my final French lesson it finally helped me to grasp the intricacies of the grammar!

## 2. Engagement apps

Engagements apps deepen understanding of a topic and support the lesson's existing structure. At primary level, these typically tend to be literacy prompts or apps for deeper research. Here are a couple of examples of great subject specific engagement apps:

**Primary literacy: Epic Citadel**

- A free app that allows the user to explore a deserted mountainside castle

- Helps to prompt students' imagination by placing them directly in a setting

**Secondary science: Elements**

- Allows students to explore the periodic table, with 3D models of each element along with information beyond the typical textbook

There is a huge amount of potential to improve learning with engagement apps, but they do require a certain level of skill from teachers to integrate them into their standard practice which is why staff development is so important.

## 3. Digital 'worksheet' apps

These are direct digital replacements for paper worksheets you already use in the classroom. Unfortunately, many of the most popular 'educational' apps fall into this category. While these apps might claim to drive up literacy standards or improve mathematical understanding, in reality they offer little, if any, functional improvement over the existing classroom activities you are likely already doing. These apps are popular, readily available and, to an extent, can make classwork appear more exciting or engaging. Consequently, we have reached a point where these digital 'worksheet' apps are the majority of what schools use. This, I would argue, is the root cause of why the iPad has had such modest impact across education as a whole; all but a few schools are yet to recognise that they are only digitising existing student tasks.

## THE CASC APPROACH

CASC stands for **C**reation, **As**sessment and **C**uration, and these are the three elements to focus on when developing your school's curriculum.

When technology revolutionises an industry, it does so from one of two bases: improvement in efficiency or improvement in process. It is time to start doing the same in education. In April 2016, I ran a survey through my company LearnMaker that asked teachers what above everything else do they want more of. Out of over three hundred responses, over 60% answered 'time'. This reflects my experience working face-to-face with teachers who are often energy-depleted and feel they have no work-life balance. Efficiency and process should be at the forefront of your mind if you are looking to improve standards in your own school. Your biggest strength is your teachers, and the more time and space you can create for them to work in, the higher their quality of teaching is likely to be. With that in mind, let's look at how the CASC framework can help you in this endeavour.

## Creation

Apps that create content can be used by teachers or students, and can impact hugely on the efficiency and processes of learning in your school. With the iPad, there is a huge variety of content-creation activities available, from movie-making, to digital book creation, to interactive presentations. Apps to look for include:

- Explain Everything
- Book Creator
- Keynote
- iMovie
- DoInk

In my view, the range of features in Explain Everything make it by far the best of these. To explain how creating content can benefit your classroom, let us have a look at this particular app in more detail.

Explain Everything is a screencasting app that enables you to draw, animate and narrate to the limits of your imagination. You record onto a digital whiteboard that can be exported into a video file. Upload that to YouTube and students can access it anywhere, at any time. This could be anything from a video demonstrating how to solve algebra equations to a presentation on the politics of the

# THE TABLET REVOLUTION

War of the Roses. In other words, students are no longer restricted to classroom-only learning. You are not just teaching history at 2.30pm on a Friday afternoon; you are teaching history whenever students want to learn! This is truly transformational, and it is the biggest leap in organised education since the invention of the printing press.

This can be particularly beneficial when teaching subjects that require conceptual understanding such as maths and sciences. Visual demonstrations are vital for students grappling with algebra, atoms or chemical bonds. By creating screencasts with Explain Everything, these demonstrations are accessible all hours of the day.

Students can also use Explain Everything to create original content. As Bloom's Taxonomy says, "The more student-centric the task, the deeper the learning" and you do not get much deeper than asking students to create original content. Instead of issuing recap tests at the end of topics, instead have students create instructional videos that cover the key concepts you wish to cement. You will easily be able to differentiate which of your students have a full grasp of the topic in question from those who require more support. All without having to mark thirty test papers!

## Assessment

If there is one area that has the potential to be transformed by apps and workflow reform, it is assessment and feedback. Marking work is commonly cited as a task that eats most into teachers' time and, put bluntly, is the bane of many educators' lives. Digitising assessment should considerably speed up the process of marking, while simultaneously deepening the level of interaction with students. Done properly, this combination is a powerful force for improving learning.

The easiest way to explain how you might digitise assessment in your school is to share my experiences working on a project with the maths department of Broadgreen International School in Liverpool. The project's aim was to improve learning within the department by changing the processes in place. When we ran this project the students were right in the middle of learning algebra for the first time.

### Case Study: Broadgreen International School

*The focus of this project was to digitise the department's marking and feedback through Showbie, a app that allows you to digitally assess work. During this project, the only person in the classroom who required an iPad was the teacher; the majority of student work was still completed on paper. The teachers took photos of students' work with their iPad and were then able to use Showbie to digitally annotate and mark it. Students would log in to Showbie on their mobiles, tablets, computers or any other device with Internet access to receive their feedback. No more need to carry boxes of exercise books home! Teachers could also use Showbie's audio and video tools to deliver deeper feedback much quicker.*

*The school's marking policy required an open dialogue between teacher and student on all submitted work: the teacher gives 'first stage' feedback, the student responds, and then the teacher issues a final summary. This process took two weeks due to the number of students and other demands on teachers' time. Digitising the process reduced the cycle to just 48 hours and allowed for more meaningful dialogue between student and teacher. Using Showbie's inbuilt messaging feature, students could ask teachers for advice on their homework quickly and easily prior to submission, and teachers were able respond to students individually or, if numerous students were asking the same questions, to an entire group. After ten weeks on the project we found the impact was significant:*

*300% increase in student teacher assessment interactions*
*98% increase in independent learning opportunities*
*86% improvement in marking turnaround time*

I often recommend that schools embracing iPads use Showbie for assessment. In my opinion, it is the best and most powerful assessment tool for tablets currently. It has plenty of competitors, but for me it mixes all the right elements in terms of ease of use, great accessibility and powerful feedback and annotation tools.

Some assume that assessment is a one-way process in which students receive feedback from teachers, but it is worth stopping to ask yourself: how does a teacher receive feedback from students? Have they understood the subject content? Did they find the learning methods helpful or not? This is where the education system is at its most outdated, because teachers only receive this kind of feedback by marking books or tests; a slow and time-intensive method. It may have been suitable a hundred years ago when teachers taught only handfuls of students, but in modern schools, teachers are responsible for hundreds and this manual system was never scalable to this level. This is where technology can bridge the gap, and by using apps such as Plickers, Kahoot, NearPod or Google Forms, teachers are able to run on-the-spot knowledge checks and exit surveys to assess their students' understanding; all without adding to their workload.

Apps to investigate at this stage:

- Showbie
- Kahoot

- Plickers
- Google Forms
- NearPod

**Curation**

In simple terms, curation is publishing to a wider audience. Providing students with an online platform on which to share their work can be a powerful motivator, because it gives it a 'real world' context and function. Some schools are sceptical about this approach, but if a student does not care what teachers think, then offering them a different and more relatable audience can make a huge difference to the quality of their work. Schools are constantly looking for new ways to engage students in learning, so before buying expensive online programmes or having motivational experts come into school, try something that is completely free of charge. Publish work online and give students something real to work towards.

The motivation does not stop once the work has been posted either. Once it is 'live' online, it is in an everlasting feedback loop. I believe that all schools should embrace YouTube because of the potential for students to interact with the online community through its commenting system. If alarm bells have already started ringing, be assured that comments can be run through a moderation process before being published, thus removing the possibility of cyber-bullying and inappropriate comments from Internet trolls.

Last year, a British Year 6 primary school class created persuasive videos to raise awareness of global warming and polar bear endangerment. They published their finished presentations to YouTube and, with a little help from their teacher's tweets, their videos reached the WWF, Al Gore, the NSPCA and PETA who left fantastic words of praise and encouragement. Just imagine how inspired those students must have been to learn the WWF had viewed and loved their work! Learning does not get more relevant and meaningful than that in my view.

Apps / Programs to look into:

- YouTube
- Vimeo
- Facebook
- Blogging (Try WordPress or Blogger to get started)

## KEY TAKEAWAYS

- Understand that not all apps are created equally. Many apps are nothing more than 'digital worksheets,' substitutions for a pen and paper task. If it does not add a functional improvement to the learning activity, it is not adding value.

- Content creation **always** trumps content consumption for students. Explain Everything is the king of all content creation. Download it today and integrate it into your teaching.

- Only part of a teacher's job takes place in the classroom. Think about what an iPad can improve in terms of paperwork, admin and planning. Marking and feedback is the biggest challenge in many schools, yet few are even considering digitising this process and reaping the rewards.

# THE TABLET REVOLUTION

# Chapter 18
# LEARNING EVOLVED

Mobile technology has democratised learning for the modern student. It is now possible to carry hours of video lectures and hundreds of textbooks on a portable device, and this means exciting new opportunities for teachers to engage with their students.

In this chapter, I will look at how schools can promote learning beyond the classroom and take an in-depth look at two of the most popular strategies in achieving this: flipped and blended learning.

## FLIPPED LEARNING

The concept behind flipped learning is straightforward. Rather than having students come 'cold' to the lesson with no prior understanding of the topic, you issue the learning material ahead of time for students to research and consume. Students then attend lessons with a level of understanding which enables the teacher to prioritise deepening that understanding. This signals a departure from the lecture-driven teaching style that has dominated education for over one hundred years, in which the primary objective of a lesson is to deliver the required information.

Numerous papers and studies from America support the notion that flipped learning has a beneficial impact on student attainment in high-stakes testing. The University of Massachusetts published a paper in 2015 called *"Design, Implementation, and Evaluation of a Flipped Format General Chemistry Course"* in which they detailed a 3 year-long study of flipped learning from their chemistry faculty. They found that students in a flipped learning environment achieved on average one grade higher than those who did not. This is a significant difference, and suggests that flipped learning warrants further exploration within the UK education.

Another benefit to flipped learning is that it improves processes within teaching; specifically, it reduces teacher paperwork. Initially, you may need to invest time to create, curate and organise the learning resources that will become the backbone of the flipped learning initiative, but once these resources are in place, teachers will save that time many times over. This is because flipped learning replaces traditional homework assignments. Imagine a work week with no piles of books to mark. This saved time can be reinvested into planning lessons or developing further flipped learning resources. Thus, a continuous cycle is established, long term, can significantly improve student attainment.

## HOW TO IMPLEMENT FLIPPED LEARNING

Flipped learning is not a change that you can implement overnight as it takes a committed staff team. For it to be a success, flipped learning in your school must keep to the basic principle that the resource you give to students requires them to research the topic prior to the lesson.

This can be more difficult than it sounds, because it requires teachers to depart from the 'lecture' style of teaching, in which they supply all the information that a student will need. If you issue resources that students simply consume, rather than those that require their own input, you risk undermining your 'flipped' environment. Materials can range from basic resources such as supplying students with a PDF, right through to the more advanced such as creating an interactive video.

Ways to start creating flipped learning resources:

- Upload PowerPoint presentations into iMovie and narrate over each slide. Export this as a video for students to refer back to
- Create PDF worksheets that include 'active' learning tasks. Set a student a challenge in which they require information that they are yet to be taught in lesson. The student must research the required information independently.
- Create screencasts, interactive videos using Explain Everything. This will allow you to include animations and visual learning examples than anything paper based.
- Challenge students to give a one minute presentation on a set topic in the next lesson. This works very well in subjects such as geography and history where information is easily accessible.

Some teachers worry that students will go away and research irrelevant information. I feel that this concern is the result of the current test-driven culture in education. It is important to remember that learning is not a linear activity. Just because you spent a 50-minute lesson teaching algebra, it does not mean everyone of your students necessarily understands it; learning happens at different rates for different individuals. Motivation and curiosity to learn are just as big determiners of academic achievement as access to knowledge is. You can give a student the best teaching and learning resources in the world, but if they do not engage with them, they do not learn. Schools should be focused on developing independent learners, students who possess motivation and curiosity to learn, and one of the best ways to start developing those skills is to begin implementing flipped learning.

## BLENDED LEARNING

Blended learning environments are those that use digital tools to 'extend' the classroom. In other words, digital content is made available for learners to consume outside lesson time. Unlike flipped learning, where you are fundamentally changing the structure of how learning takes place, blended learning is more of a 'top-up' process whereby students gain access to more content to help them deepen their understanding of the subject. Here are some platforms on which you can build a blended learning environment.

### 1. iTunes U

iTunes U is what is termed a MOOC (a Massive Open Online Course), an app that allows students to digest content independently of the course leader. The course leader can either allow content to be viewed at specific times or release all material at once so that students have the option of learning ahead of time. In the schools I have worked with using this system, students who had access to all the course content tended to consume it faster than in a traditional classroom-only environment. Greg Hughes, project leader at The de Ferrers Academy, backs this up and also states that he is seeing students achieve higher grades through the use of iTunes U.

One prerequisite of iTunes U is that each student must have an iPad to access content. This is why having a long term vision and strategy is critical, because the hardware requirements mean that almost no schools are in a position to implement iTunes U immediately. This requires a commitment and significant investment into iPads, but if you are prepared to take that leap, then iTunes U has many advantages. The first is that the iTunes U platform houses all course and learning materials, videos, PDFs and even links to required apps. There is even a notes function built into the platform to allow students to record their ideas.

## 2. iBooks

iBooks is Apple's digital book store and allows you access to its range of digital textbooks. Just to be clear, iBooks are different to eBooks, the text files that you can download onto an Amazon

Kindle. iBooks are interactive and support not only pictures and videos, but also widgets, including quizzes and 3D models. It's science books, for example include videos of chemical reactions and 3D models of the molecules involved in the process. The rich content of this resource allows students to engage with their learning material at a deeper level.

To make the most of iBooks' potential, I recommend downloading iBooks Author, a free program that teachers can use to create their own books (only available on Mac). By creating your own curriculum content and publishing it to iBooks, you can create bespoke resources specifically for your students' needs. I am a big fan of schools that take this approach. ESSA Academy and The de Ferrers Academy have both led the way and published iBook GCSE & A Level courses for their students. Project leaders Abdul Chohan and Greg Hughes attribute these resources to aiding to the improvement of test results.

Publishing your intellectual property to a global platform will also help to boost your school's reputation and profile locally. This is exactly what Cambridge-based independent school The Stephen Perse Foundation, found when they were covered by BBC News for releasing all of their iBooks courses to the public free of charge.

## 3. Udemy

The final option is for those who want to develop blended learning content but do not want to be tied to Apple's ecosystem. Udemy is an online learning platform, primarily driven by video content, that is accessible from any Internet browser. This is a big advantage for schools who may not have enough iPads to commit to iTunes U or iBooks, but who still want to begin implementing blended learning.

Udemy is a great option in this scenario as it is free and web based, meaning students can access the content from any number of devices. Creating a Udemy course is quite straightforward, as the content is grouped into modules. The drawback is that Udemy is video driven, and although you are able to upload text or PDF documents, these are displayed within a slide show style browser. Documents can be downloadable but this resembles a more fragmented approach to learning resources, like that of a VLE system rather than the more immersive iTunes U and iBooks platforms.

To get the real benefits from Udemy requires content to be curated by a presenter in front of the camera, so be prepared to put in a bit of extra time and effort for this. If you do, I am sure you will reap the rewards.

## FINDING THE TIME TO DEVELOP CONTENT

Time is a school's most precious resource, and one of the biggest challenges you will face when trying to introduce blended or flipped learning is finding space in your schedule to create content in the initial stages. If you can persevere in the short term with the extra work, you will reap the long-term rewards once it is complete. Here are some tips to help you find time:

**1. Prioritise one department**

Prioritise developing resources for the subject in your school with the most pressing need. This is a strategy I have employed with numerous schools because that subject will demand more meetings, planning, administration and floor walks than others. If you can improve the performance of your worst performing department, you will find that it frees up countless hours, which you can then reinvest into the next department that needs help, and step by step you will raise the performance of each, saving numerous hours along the way.

**2. Work collectively**

Many hands make light work, and this is never more true than when developing learning resources. Your iPad team should delegate the responsibility of gathering and creating the content to the department in question. Next, they need to work with that department and allocate individual responsibilities for specific topics. Creating a biology GCSE iTunes U course is a huge undertaking for one person, but if you have eight teachers working collectively on set modules, then that task is no longer so overwhelming. Once the course is complete, put it in the hands of a good editor to ensure quality control and before you know it you have developed your first blended learning course.

## 3. Repurpose existing content

Do not abandon what has always worked in the classroom for what is new. The iPad offers some really immersive learning opportunities, but substance always wins over style. Across your department, you already have all the content you will need to create blended learning courses. This means the hardest part is already taken care of! The only work needed is in selecting what materials and content to use, and how you can take advantage of interactive opportunities by adding pictures, videos or quizzes to augment learning further.

## 4. Set manageable time schedules

Do a little each day rather than a lot once per week. I wrote this book by sitting down and writing 500 words per day; the key was that 500 words a day was manageable for my time schedule. Stick to what is manageable. Set up scheduled meetings within the department to ensure everyone is on track and to give additional support in case anyone is struggling.

## 5. Crowdsource

If you do need to create new content but cannot find the time, why not call upon your students to help? There is a student-led teaching and learning approach called *'mantle of the expert'* that was pioneered by Professor Dorothy Heathcoate in the 1980s. It was originally created to redevelop learning through the use of creative drama by allowing students to dictate teaching and learning, and I have seen it applied to mobile technology learning to equally great effect.

Allocating expertise to students by challenging them to create publishable content is a powerful motivator. This can be achieved as easily as tasking students to create a recap video at the end of a topic. It is a great opportunity for students to cement and evaluate their own knowledge, but it also gives you a choice of numerous resources that can be reused at a later date.

## 6. Off-set costs

If you have tried all of the suggestions above and still cannot find the time their is a final option open to you: hire someone to create the course. This is exactly what The Stephen Perse Foundation did when developing blended resources for every subject in their school. Once your course is finished, the school can reap the financial benefits. These include:

- A reduction in the need to buy or replace textbooks.
- A reduction in photocopying costs, which can amount to thousands of pounds per year minimum.
- A reduction in the requirement of printing facilities, which can amount to thousands of pounds per year on long term lease agreements.
- The ability to review and reduce what learning resources need to be bought.
- A reduction in spend on student as students' performance improves.

I have seen first hand how much money a school can save when its resources are managed smartly. Investing time and money in blended learning, even to the extent of hiring a dedicated employee to manage its development, is a move that will pay itself back in no time.

## KEY TAKEAWAYS

- iPads excel when students have access to resources, and the quicker you can get a blended / flipped learning environment up and running the bigger the impact you will likely see.

- Curriculum development, in its true form is about developing what you already have. It may be nice to add new apps and activities into your repertoire but these should build upon what you already do. Following this simple rule will enable you to implement technology at a faster, and more impactful rate than if you throw a bunch of new apps into your teaching practice.

- Teamwork wins the day. Work collaboratively with other teachers to create deep and insightful material to support your department. You can't transform a department with a new worksheet, but you can with a bespoke course. Work together and share the workload, and with just a few hours sacrifice each week you will soon have a bespoke department resource that trumps even the best downloadable worksheet.

# THE TABLET REVOLUTION

# Chapter 19
# MEASURING SUCCESS

Measuring impact might come fairly low down on your priorities once you find yourself in the swing of an iPad project. You already have your iPad team to organise, suppliers to choose and workflow to reorganise. It may sound like extra work, but I recommend you take the time to take data and evaluate the difference your project has made. It will help you to understand what has been successful, what areas of learning and pedagogy have improved, and how the project can be tweaked to ensure even better outcomes going forward. Done the right way, this need not be a lengthy or time-consuming task.

To make things easier, you want to choose indicators that are relatively easy to measure and will provide you with reliable information about how well your project is going. There are many to pick from, but to give you an idea of how you might approach measuring impact, I want to use this chapter to focus on just four:

- Engagement
- Instruction quality
- Access to content
- Enjoyment

## ENGAGEMENT

When it comes to student engagement, appearances can be deceiving. Students might be sitting quietly in their chairs with their eyes on you, and yet be a million miles away. Likewise, if you ask how engaged they feel with a subject, you may find students who appear uninterested rating themselves as '100% engaged'. Students can be skilled at giving the answers you want to hear! To get to the bottom of how much your iPad project has impacted on engagement, it is important to look at the data your school already collects and see what differences there are since the project began. The clues are in attendance and behaviour!

**Attendance:** If your iPad project is going well, then attendance should begin to improve as the project progresses. By deploying iPads to year groups or subjects, rather than a 'bookable resource' model, you will find it very simple to contrast the year-on-year attendance data. Contrast attendance over a long time frame to account for any short term variances.

**Behaviour:** If your school already collects data on behaviour, it can be a treasure trove of insight. If students are more engaged in their learning, there should be fewer incidents of misbehaviour. Hove Park School in East Sussex, for example, saw a huge reduction in instances of misbehaviour in classrooms after the introduction of iPads, and now have one of the most successful projects in the UK.

It is worth stopping to consider the snowball effect this creates. With fewer behaviour interruptions in the lesson the average learning time per lesson increases. This may not sound like a game changer, but if your average teacher spends five minutes more each lesson teaching and supporting students instead of managing behaviour, then this quickly accumulates. I am painting in broad strokes here to illustrate the potential, but if there is an extra five minutes teaching per class across five lessons per day, over a school year this adds up to 4000 minutes. That is an additional 66 hours of teaching time.

## INSTRUCTION QUALITY

How effectively is teacher feedback aiding students to develop? I covered this topic in detail in the Apps and Workflow chapter under the Digitising Assessment for Learning section. In terms of measuring its impact there are two easy indicators.

**Turnaround time:** How long does it take for a student to get a piece of work marked and returned? Immediacy of feedback is an important, yet forgotten aspect of learning in schools. Many marking cycles take up to two weeks to complete, meaning that in core subjects students may have had anywhere up to ten lessons in that subject go by. The curriculum has already moved students on, so how valuable is it giving them feedback still?

For turnaround time you can contrast the marking cycle before iPads were introduced and with iPads.

**Depth of interaction:** the more interactions a teacher and student have over a piece of submitted work, the more opportunities to improve learning.

On a paper based marking cycle, interactions are typically capped at three:

- Teacher comments on submitted work
- Student responds to teacher's comments
- Teacher leaves final comments

On a digital based marking cycle the interaction cap is lifted.

With the use of an app like Showbie, teacher and student can interact far more over a standard marking cycle. I saw this firsthand with Broadgreen International School where average interactions through the marking cycle increased from 3 to 9. I view feedback to improve learning much like archery whereby you are trying to hit a target. Each interaction with a student brings the target a step closer, and increases the chance that you will hit the bullseye.

## ACCESS TO CONTENT

The more opportunities for learning that can take place outside of school the better. This is an easy category to measure because it is yes or no.

- Can students access classroom material outside of the lesson?
- Can students access curriculum material ahead of the lesson?

Whether you are sending iPads home or developing a blended learning environment, the important aspect to keep in mind is that learning opportunities increase when students can access material outside of school.

## ENJOYMENT

People of all ages, whether children or adults tend to perform better when they enjoy what they do. School should not be a chore for students and staff, and often it is processes, not content that is driving dislike. I have worked with many schools where we have prioritised enjoyment, and with a little tweak of a few aspects you can gain a huge positive swing in your favour.

The best way to measure enjoyment is to run an anonymous survey for teachers and students. It always proves to be an excellent barometer of how individual subjects are performing, and where exactly the challenges and barriers to improvement are. Google Forms enables you to collect and collate data easily, and this task is best undertaken by asking respondents to rate statements such as 'I enjoy history...' on a sliding scale of 1-5, and by following this up with open ended questions such as:

- What do I like about the subject?
- What do I dislike about the subject?
- What would help me learn better?

## KEY TAKEAWAYS

- You cannot drive improvements if you do not have the data. It is vital that you measure and contrast performance in areas other than test results. Results are the final outcome of a whole host of smaller factors in schools. Get the small factors right and the results will eventually follow.

- Do you know what students actually think of subjects? Enjoyment has a huge impact on student performance, and often things that are driving down enjoyment are within your power to remove.

- Run anonymous staff and student surveys throughout the year to really gauge the effectiveness of your project, as well as to uncover the day to day challenges, frustrations and barriers each group is facing. The more challenges you can uncover, the quicker you can resolve them and help your project move forward.

# THE TABLET REVOLUTION

# TYING IT ALL TOGETHER

If there is one thing I want you to take away from this book, it is that the project you are about to embark on is **yours**, and unique to your school. There is no one-size-fits-all model that I can offer you, because each school is different. Focus your project on a vision that factors in all the needs, strengths and weaknesses that are particular to your organisation. It is valuable to learn from those who have gone before you, but any attempt to copy and paste will result in mediocre results at best.

Remember that there is no such thing as overnight success. The likes of ESSA Academy, The de Ferrers Academy and Hove Park achieved their success through years of careful planning and hard work. They did not shy away from the task before them and, in taking the time to think through and prepare for the challenges that lay ahead of them, addressed all of the areas covered in this book with great skill.

Whether you are about to buy your first set of school iPads or your school already has a project underway, you have a commonality with every other educator exploring technology in their classroom. You are all on a journey to transform learning for the better.

I wrote this book because I want every school to take advantage of the learning opportunities that the iPad affords teachers and learners, and to be able to avoid the pitfalls that have hampered so many projects in the past. The cycle of committing huge sums of money to technology without also committing to the process to ensure it is impactful must be stopped. The schools of today find themselves in the greatest democratisation of learning there has ever been, and although technology can **accelerate** a transformation it cannot **cause** a transformation. Transformation is the realm of the teacher, and everything in your iPad project must be set up to support that.

# REFERENCES

Anderson, L. W. and Krathwohl, D. R., et al (2001) A Taxonomy for Learning, Teaching, and Assessing: A Revision of Bloom's Taxonomy of Educational Objectives

Bloom, B.S. and Krathwohl, D. R. (1956) Taxonomy of Educational Objectives: The Classification of Educational Goals

Burden, K, et al. (2012) iPad Scotland Evaluation

Clarke, B. et al. (2015), Transforming Learning; Ethnographic observations and interviews

Department of Children, Schools and Families. (2008) The Impact of Parental Involvement on Children's Education

Heathcoate, D. & Bolton, G. (1995) Drama for Learning: Dorothy Heathcoate's Mantle of the Expert Approach to Education

Kurtz, G. and Tsimerman, A., et al (2014) The Flipped Classroom Approach: The Answer to Future Learning?

Marlowe, C, A. (2012) The Effect of The Flipped Classroom on Student Achievement and Stress

OECD. (2015) Students, Computers and Learning: Making the Connection

Puentedura, R. (2013) SAMR Model: Six Exemplars

Shulman, L. (1986) The TPACK Model

Tecknowledge (2014), The Use of Tablets in UK Schools: A Research Report

The Stages of Learning Cycle (also known as The Four Stages of Competence), originally developed by Noel Burch of Gordon Training International in the 1970s

The Sutton Trust (2015) Developing Teachers: Improving Professional Development for Teachers

The Teacher Development Trust (2014), Developing Great Teaching: Lessons from the international reviews into effective professional

The University of Massachusetts. (2015) Design, Implementation, and Evaluation of a Flipped Format General Chemistry Course

Weaver, G. & Sturtevant, H. (2015) Design, Implementation, and Evaluation of a Flipped Format General Chemistry Course

# ACKNOWLEDGEMENTS

I'd like to say a huge thanks to all the people who've helped make this book possible, especially my perfect partner in life and creativity Charlotte Green. What started out as Charlotte spending a few hours each week helping me to edit my writing quickly evolved into co-authoring with me, and the book became all the richer for it. Without Charlotte's support, motivation and input the book you have just read simply wouldn't exist!

Secondly a huge thankyou to James Hannam, one of my closest friends and business partner. What a journey we've been on! From that first hectic day we spent together all those years ago in Colchester battling to unbox and deploy 400 iPads in just a few hours to running LearnMaker together now. Long may the adventure continue!

In my career I'd like to say a big thankyou to Phil Harrison, my first manager at Apple and Martin Lomas, my first sales manager at GBM, both of whose philosophies and principals taught me that sales is all about personal relationships and conversations. I'd also like to thank both Manny Figueira and Neil Douglas, two of the most immensely knowledgeable and experienced professionals I've had the pleasure to work with. Thankyou both for answering my endless questions when we worked together!

Finally I'd like to thank my book launch team for helping spread the word about this book in a true grass roots effort. If you picked this book up from Amazon or somewhere else you have these guys to thank for building the momentum:

Racher Smith, Neelam Parmar, Martin Coutts, Ian Simpson, James South, Johnny Slater, Thomasin Bailey, Kjell Senumsted, Glyn Rozier, Thomas Røst Stenerud, Stuart James Bush, Steven Caldwell, Danielle Basker, Tamar Kopperl Simpson, Elisabeth Palmgren, James Diamond, Janita Paulsen, Wendy MacGregor, Andy Fawkes, David Hamill, Laura Mumby-Croft, Kevin Burden, Steve Woodhouse, Gareth Nichols, Jana Craig Hare, Ali Carr, Diana Moule, Colin James Grimes, Isabella Macquarries, Laura Setterfield, Dawn Pirle, Sarah Rhia Owen, Mike Watson, Sam William, Helen Caldwell, Calum Race, Rebecca Leighton, Nigel Pantling, Jamie Payne, Hambo Mackenzie, Leif Henrik Kobbeltvedt, Linzie Stephenson.

# ABOUT THE AUTHOR

Jay Ashcroft is cofounder of LearnMaker, a school leadership and development company that lends a platform to his successful corporate world experience and passion for education. In 2010, Jay was selected to join Apple and lead a new store in a destination location in the North of England, training and developing a team of over 50 staff members. Taking the store from inception to one of the top performers in Europe in his first 12 months, Jay went on to support the rollout of new stores across the Northern territory, lead training sessions at the annual countrywide conference and establish a training programme for new employees.

Moving into the education technology sector, Jay was recruited to establish and develop a Northern territory for a national Apple reseller, bringing best in class service and support to education institutions across the North of England. When Jay left two years later, he had overseen over £2 million of Apple technology deployed into schools and worked with thousands of teachers.

In 2014, dissatisfied with how little technology was improving schools, he left his lucrative career behind to set up his first company, LearnMaker. Reflecting on his time at Apple, he realised that the environment and culture of an organisation is a bigger determiner of performance than its budgets or people, and that there is no reason why this philosophy can't be applied with equal success in schools.

Today, Jay works with school leaders to develop high performing cultures that bring about better results, improve efficiency and make leading a school a much more enjoyable process. His work to date has seen him nominated for the prestigious NAACE Impact Award, invited onto a three year Europe wide project to improve teaching pedagogies and become a regular speaker at education conferences.

His belief is that every school can develop their own high performing culture and his mission is to make that a reality.

# LEARNMAKER DEVELOPMENT PROGRAMME

The key to excelling with technology is to have the right culture within your school to enable you to take advantage of it. If you are interested in working with us to develop a high performing culture then our cultural development programme might be right for you.

You can learn more about what this programme 'typically' looks like at **www.learnmaker.co.uk**

I say 'typically' because we know that your school is unique, and we tailor our work to each and every school to ensure it is of the highest quality. Our website will show you what works in most schools but we understand that one size doesn't fit all.

## HEAR FROM REAL SCHOOL LEADERS FIRST HAND

If you want to hear from school leaders who have recently developed high performing cultures within their own schools you can find their videos at:

www.youtube.com/learnmakeruk

## ANNUAL CONFERENCE

Come along to our annual school leadership conference where you will hear from great headteachers and meet many others who are striving to develop a high performing culture in their own school.

You will find more details at www.learnmaker.co.uk. Make sure to register your interest in attending because it sells out quickly.

## HOW TO CONTACT LEARNMAKER

We would love to hear from you so feel free to get in touch via:

www.learnmaker.co.uk

hello@learnmaker.co.uk

## PLUS...

Jay is giving away **free tickets** and samples of his new products to everyone who reviews this book!

Jay Ashcroft's company LearnMaker regularly hosts events, webinars, discussions, strategy sessions and much more. To see what's coming up visit **www.learnmaker.co.uk**

So, if you would like to review this book, we will reward you for taking the time to do so. Here's how:

1. Write a review of this book
2. Post it on Amazon, iTunes Bookstore, your blog, your Facebook page, or get it published in another publication
3. Send a link or screenshot to **hello@learnmaker.co.uk**
4. You will be sent free tickets to upcoming events or receive samples of new products and services from LearnMaker (depending on where you are and what we have going on at the time)

Thanks for reading **THE TABLET REVOLUTION!**

Printed in Great Britain
by Amazon